LONDON 1914–17

The Zeppelin Menace

CAMPAIGN • 193

LONDON 1914–17

The Zeppelin Menace

IAN CASTLE

ILLUSTRATED BY CHRISTA HOOK

Series editors Marcus Cowper and Nikolai Bogdanovic

First published in Great Britain in 2008 by Osprey Publishing,
Midland House, West Way, Botley, Oxford OX2 0PH, UK
44-02 23rd St, Suite 219, Long Island City, NY 11101, USA
Email: info@ospreypublishing.com

Osprey Publishing is part of the Osprey Group.

Transferred to digital print on demand 2011

First published 2008
2nd impression 2009

Printed and bound by PrintOnDemand-Worldwide.com, Peterborough, UK

A CIP catalogue record for this book is available from the British Library

ISBN 978 184603 245 5

Editorial by Ilios Publishing Ltd, Oxford, UK (www.iliospublishing.com)
Page layout by The Black Spot
Index by Peter Rea
Maps by the Map Studio Ltd.
Battlescene illustrations by Christa Hook
Originated by PDQ Digital Media Solutions Ltd.
Typeset in Myriad Pro and Sabon

Dedication
For Colin, Mike, Martin, Steve and Will – old soldiers one and all.

Acknowledgements
My interest in the Zeppelin raids on London was first fuelled by a rather
dilapidated plaque on the wall of a building in Farringdon Road,
Clerkenwell. It commemorates a raid that took place on 8 September
1915, and, although I have lived in London all my life, it made me realize
that I knew little of this period in the city's history. The journey from that
point to the completion of this book has been a fascinating one. One
made easier thanks to the methodical work of the anonymous clerks of
the Royal Flying Corps, Royal Naval Air Service, Metropolitan Police and
London Fire Brigade, who diligently filed away the countless reports and
documents that can today be freely consulted at the National Archives in
Kew, London. In particular, the maps, that are an important feature of this
book, would not have been possible without their efforts. To these people
I am deeply indebted.

I must also express my gratitude to my good friend Colin Ablett, who
gave me access to his library and granted permission to use illustrations
from his collection. I would also like to thank Becky Latchford of the
Essex Police Museum for permission to use a photograph from their
collection and to Martin Atkinson of the National Trust who obtained
permission for me to visit the crash site of Zeppelin L.33 in Essex. Unless
otherwise stated, all photographs in the book are from my own collection.

Finally, I must acknowledge the contribution of Christa Hook to this
project. Once again, she has taken my sketchiest of sketches and turned
them into magnificent works of art.

EQUIVALENT RANKS & ABBREVIATIONS

German rank	Abbreviation	British Rank	Abbreviation
Navy			
Fregattenkapitän	–	Captain	Capt
Korvettenkapitän	Kvtkpt	Commander	Cdr
Kapitänleutnant	Kptlt	Lieutenant-Commander	Lt-Cdr
Oberleutnant-zur-See	Oblt-z-S	Lieutenant	Lt
Army			
Oberst	–	Colonel	Col
Oberstleutnant	–	Lieutenant-Colonel	Lt-Col
Major	Maj	Major	Maj
Hauptmann	Hptmn	Captain	Capt
Oberleutnant	Oblt	Lieutenant	Lt

Imperial War Museum collections
Some of the photos in this book come from the Imperial War Museum's
huge collections which cover all aspects of conflict involving Britain
and the Commonwealth since the start of the twentieth century.
These rich resources are available online to search, browse and buy at
www.iwmcollections.org.uk. In addition to Collections Online, you can
visit the Visitor Rooms where you can explore over 8 million photographs,
thousands of hours of moving images, the largest sound archive of its
kind in the world, thousands of diaries and letters written by people in
wartime, and a huge reference library. To make an appointment, call
(020) 7416 5320, or e-mail: mail@iwm.org.uk.

Imperial War Museum www.iwm.org.uk

The Woodland Trust
Osprey Publishing is supporting the Woodland Trust, the UK's leading
woodland conservation charity, by funding the dedication of trees.

www.ospreypublishing.com

CONTENTS

INTRODUCTION

Ferdinand von Zeppelin (1838–1917). Zeppelin retired from the army in 1891 and concentrated on airship development. In 1900 he launched his first steerable rigid airship, based on original designs of aviation pioneer David Schwarz, who had died three years earlier.

The rapid descent to war experienced in the hot summer of 1914 alerted scaremongers in Britain to the threat of immediate aerial bombardment of London and other major industrial cities. The publicity and propaganda surrounding the development of Germany's fleet of airships spread far and wide, and the spectre of these great leviathans of the air sowing the seeds of death and destruction in the streets of London suddenly became very real.

Two days after Britain declared war on Germany, the editor of *The Times* newspaper informed his readers that the enemy boasted a force of 11 airships serving with their armed forces – but, he claimed reassuringly, only two were capable of reaching Britain. The following day, 7 August, preparations for the air defence of London began when a single, unarmed aircraft took up station at Hendon, a suburb north-west of the city. The next day, the Admiralty added to the defence by assigning three guns to anti-aircraft duties in Whitehall, close to the seat of government. But no attack materialized. In fact, nine months would pass before German airships finally hovered menacingly over the streets of London. Even then, Britain had little answer to the threat, and not until the late summer of 1916 could the armed forces offer a serious and deadly response.

THE ROAD TO WAR

The father of rigid airship development was Count Ferdinand von Zeppelin. Others had experimented with the principles of lighter-than-air flight, but it was Zeppelin whose *Luftschiff* (airship) *Zeppelin 1* first took to the air on 2 July 1900. It would be another three years before the Wright brothers coaxed their flimsy Wright Flyer into the air for the first manned, controlled and powered flight by a heavier-than-air machine. However, these early tentative skyward leaps marked the first milestones on the journey that brought airship and aeroplane to battle over the hushed and darkened streets of London just 12 years later.

Count Zeppelin built further models, and despite a number of setbacks he persevered and engendered massive support from the German people. The German military began to take notice too and in 1909 the army purchased two airships, numbering them Z.I and Z.II.[1] After a period of evaluation, the army ordered two more airships from the Zeppelin Company. Not to be outdone, the navy placed its first order in April 1912 with a second

1 For more information on the complex issue of German airship nomenclature, see Osprey New Vanguard 101: *Zeppelins: German Airships 1900–40*.

following in 1913. However, the Zeppelin Company was not the only builder of airships. In 1909 a rival company set up business. Fronted by Johann Schütte, Professor of Naval Architecture at Danzig University, and funded principally by an industrialist, Karl Lanz, Luftschiffbau Schütte-Lanz GmbH built its first airship in 1911 before selling its second model, *SL.2*, to the army in 1914.

Although more streamlined, Schütte-Lanz airships were not vastly dissimilar in appearance to the Zeppelin, although there was one significant structural difference. While the Zeppelin Company based construction on a latticed aluminium framework – later replaced by duralumin, an aluminium alloy – those of Schütte-Lanz utilized laminated plywood. However, this wooden construction did not find favour with senior naval officers, who considered it liable to catastrophic failure under continual exposure to moisture in operations over the North Sea. As such, Schütte-Lanz airships were generally more favoured by the army. But to those on the ground looking up in awe and wonder as these vast dirigibles (steerable airships) passed overhead, all airships were simply 'Zeppelins'. At the start of the war Germany possessed 11 airships, as the editor of *The Times* correctly noted: ten commanded by the army, and one by the navy.

In Britain, concern over Germany's airship programme grew, until in 1908 the government authorized an examination of the threat posed by airships and of the advantage Britain might gain from their use. As a result, Britain began a programme to build her own rigid airship, hoping to evaluate this threat in practical ways. The resultant airship, *R1 'The Mayfly'*, was short-lived, like its namesake in nature, wrecked by a squall in September 1911 before she ever flew. At the same time aeroplane development was gradually advancing. The first recognized aeroplane flight in Britain took place in October 1908. Then, the following year, Louis Blériot made his dramatic flight across the Channel.

Gradually the military turned their attention towards aviation. In April 1911 the Balloon Section of the Royal Engineers disbanded to reform as the Air Battalion while their headquarters at Farnborough was renamed the

Following Blériot's dramatic crossing of the English Channel, H.G. Wells commented that Britain, from a military viewpoint, was no longer 'an inaccessible island'. This was also appreciated in Germany, as this propaganda postcard shows.

The German people responded enthusiastically to Count Zeppelin's work. After the loss of *LZ.4* in a fire in 1908, the public donated some 6 million marks to enable him to continue development. This influx of funds enabled Count Zeppelin to continue developing more powerful craft and financed the creation of the Deutsche Luftschiffahrts-Aktien-Gesellschaft (DELAG), the world's first commercial airline. DELAG airships soon became a common sight, roving over the German countryside offering pleasure cruises to the public. They subsequently ventured beyond the boundaries of Germany, into Austria and Switzerland, proudly displaying this great feat of German engineering. The population was entranced, the Zeppelin becoming a national icon and a highly visible focus for patriotism.

Army Aircraft Factory. The Royal Navy also began experimenting with aircraft, and a year later these efforts by both organizations were concentrated in a single Royal Flying Corps (RFC), with a military wing, a naval wing, a flying school at Upavon in Wiltshire and the base at Farnborough, renamed again as the Royal Aircraft Factory. However, it soon became clear that the imposed relationship between the army and navy flyers was an uneasy one. Despite the army upholding its traditional responsibility to protect the homeland, the military wing revealed in June 1914, on the eve of war, that there was still no aerial home defence organization and further more all existing squadrons were committed to providing aerial reconnaissance for any British Expeditionary Force (BEF) destined for Europe. After an uneasy relationship lasting just two years, the naval wing left the RFC to set up its own independent organization governed directly by the Admiralty and named the Royal Naval Air Service (RNAS). Shortly after the commencement of the war, the Admiralty formally accepted responsibility for the home defence tasks it had already been performing.

As the clouds of war gathered, both the RFC and RNAS gradually increased their strength, acquiring a diverse range of aircraft with which to fight this very first war in the air. The next four years witnessed remarkable advancements in aviation – yet despite its great promise, the Zeppelin failed to deliver the anticipated killer blow.

The Central Flying School opened in 1912 at Upavon in Wiltshire. Its role was to produce pilots for a wartime role from flyers already holding a Royal Aero Club Certificate. 93 pilots had successfully passed through Upavon by the beginning of the war.

CHRONOLOGY

1914

5 September   Winston Churchill, First Lord of the Admiralty, outlines his Home Defence plan as the Admiralty accepts responsibility for the aerial defence of London.

1 October   Instructions for the implementation of a blackout come into effect.

1915

9 January   Kaiser Wilhelm gives approval for air attacks on Britain – but excludes London as a target.

19/20 January   Navy Zeppelin *L.3* drops bombs on Great Yarmouth, Norfolk, during the first air raid on Britain.

12 February   The Kaiser includes London Docks in legitimate targets.

3 April   The Army Airship Service takes delivery of the first of the new P-class Zeppelins – *LZ.38*

5 May   Kaiser Wilhelm approves London 'east of the Tower of London' as a legitimate target area.

31 May/1 June   Army Zeppelin *LZ.38* makes the first airship raid on London.

6/7 June   Flight Sub-Lt R.A.J. Warneford (RNAS) destroys army Zeppelin *LZ.37* over Belgium.

20 July   Unrestricted bombing of London is approved by the Kaiser.

17/18 August   Navy Zeppelin *L.10* bombs Walthamstow, Leyton, Leytonstone and Wanstead.

7/8 September   Army airships *SL.2* and *LZ.74* bomb south-east London.

8/9 September   Navy Zeppelin *L.13*, on a course from Bloomsbury to Liverpool Street Station, causes the most material damage of all the airship raids on London.

12 September   Admiral Sir Percy Scott appointed commander of London's gunnery defence.

13/14 October   Three navy Zeppelins (*L.13*, *L.14* and *L.15*) attack London and outskirts. Bombs fall from Covent Garden to Aldgate as well as on Woolwich and East Croydon, creating the highest casualties from a single raid.

1916

10 February   Responsibility for the aerial defence of London passes from the navy to the army.

31 March/ 1 April   Navy Zeppelin *L.15* is brought down by anti-aircraft fire in the sea north of Margate, Kent.

15 April   No. 19 Reserve Aeroplane Squadron reformed as No. 39 (Home Defence) Squadron and concentrated on the north-eastern approaches to London.

15 May   RFC places the first large-scale order for Brock explosive ammunition.

30 May   The first of the R-class Super Zeppelins – *L.30* – is commissioned into navy service.

24/25 August   Navy Zeppelin *L.31* attacks the Isle of Dogs, Greenwich, Eltham and Plumstead.

2/3 September   Army airship *SL.11* is the first to be shot down over mainland Britain.

23/24 September   In a raid by navy Zeppelins, *L.33* is brought down at Little Wigborough, Essex, after bombing East London. *L.32* is shot down near Billericay, Essex. *L.31* bombs Streatham, Brixton and Leyton.

1/2 October   *L.31* is shot down over Potters Bar, Hertfordshire.

1917

28 February   *L.42*, the first of the S-class Zeppelins – the Height Climbers – is commissioned into naval service.

13 June   The first successful daylight raid on London by twin-engined Gotha bombers.

16/17 June   The S-class Zeppelin *L.48* is shot down over Theberton, Suffolk during a failed raid on London.

19/20 October   Navy Zeppelin *L.45* bombs Hendon, Cricklewood, Piccadilly, Camberwell and Hither Green in the last airship raid on London.

1918

5 August   Führer der Luftschiffe Peter Strasser is killed when *L.70* is shot down off the Norfolk coast.

OPPOSING FORCES

Winston Churchill (1874–1965). Churchill took up the post of First Lord of the Admiralty in 1911 and continued until May 1915. He was an enthusiastic supporter of aviation development and was the prime mover in establishing London's earliest aerial defence. Churchill, for one, did not see a future for the Zeppelin, describing it once as 'this enormous bladder of combustible and explosive gas' and labelling them 'gaseous monsters'. For some time, though, it looked as if he had misjudged their potential, but by the end of the war the military career of the Zeppelin was over. (I. Knight)

OPPOSING COMMANDERS

First Lord of the Admiralty, Winston S. Churchill

While Home Secretary, Churchill displayed a keen interest in naval development, leading to his appointment as First Lord of the Admiralty in October 1911. Fascinated too by the developing science of aviation, he enrolled for flying lessons in 1913. Although senior army figures saw the future of aircraft in a purely passive reconnaissance role, Churchill quickly recognized its offensive potential.

In November 1913, casting a wary eye at German airship development, Churchill expressed the need for a fighting aeroplane designed for home service. He was also a prime mover in the separation of the naval wing from the Royal Flying Corps and the formation of the RNAS. On 29 July 1914 he decreed that naval aircraft should regard defence against aerial attack their prime responsibility and expressed his opinion that London, the Woolwich Arsenal as well as the naval dockyards at Chatham and Portsmouth were all prime targets for attack. Then, in September 1914, with the RFC in Belgium with the BEF, Churchill officially accepted responsibility for home defence on behalf of the Admiralty. At a time when many were still coming to terms with this new danger from the skies, Churchill created the initial defence of Britain against aerial attack, with his first line of defence centred on the RNAS squadron based at Dunkirk in France. He also demanded that pilots based at the RNAS airfield at Hendon step into the unknown and learn to fly at night.

In January 1915, Churchill outlined the latest plans for London's defence, asserting that within the London–Sheerness–Dover triangle about 60 rifle-armed aeroplanes were permanently on stand-by to repel air invaders, adding, bullishly, that some pilots were even prepared to charge Zeppelins in the air! However, Churchill was not to oversee their final demise. As chief architect of the disastrous Gallipoli campaign he was removed from office in May 1915.

Major-General David Henderson, RFC

After army service in the Sudan in 1898, Henderson served in the Anglo-Boer War as an intelligence officer under Sir George White, enduring the siege of Ladysmith. From October 1900 to September 1902 he served under Lord Kitchener as director of military intelligence, and on his return from the war Henderson published highly respected books on intelligence and reconnaissance.

Confirming his reputation as an adventurous spirit, Henderson gained his pilot's licence in 1911 at the age of 49. He immediately developed a strong belief in the future of air power. In September 1913, having been selected to represent the army in discussions on the development of aviation, he was appointed Director-General of Military Aeronautics at the War Office, exerting control over all aspects of the military wing of the RFC – recruitment, training and equipment.

On the outbreak of war in 1914, Henderson went to France as head of the RFC. However, the rapid expansion of the organization combined with the workload generated as director of military aviation affected his health, and in August 1915 he handed over control at the front to Brigadier-General Hugh Trenchard and returned to the War Office. He faced much criticism for the failure of the RFC to stop the Zeppelin raids on London in 1915, but he persevered, developing the RFC until it was able to defeat the enemy raiders. Towards the end of the war he also played a hugely important role in the amalgamation of the RFC and RNAS into a single Royal Air Force in April 1918.

Major-General David Henderson, RFC (1862–1921). A former army intelligence officer, in 1911 (aged 49) he learned to fly, making him the world's oldest pilot at that time. He joined the RFC in 1913 as Director of Military Aeronautics.

Konteradmiral Paul Behncke

As the Deputy Chief of the German Naval Staff, Behncke became one of the most vociferous supporters for a bombing campaign against London. As early as August 1914, following the advance of the German army into Belgium, Behncke proposed the construction of airship bases on the Belgian coast to facilitate raids against Britain.

Yet Behncke's proposals met opposition at the highest level, from Kaiser Wilhelm II. With his close ties to the British royal family and his genuine belief, shared by so many others, that the war would be soon over, the Kaiser forbade the bombing of Britain. Despite this, Behncke continued to press for an air campaign, preparing a proposal for the bombing of targets in London, as well as remarking on the morale effects of bombing raids on Liverpool and Manchester too. The army and navy began discussing airship raids in October 1914, yet in reality it was not only the opposition of the Kaiser that prevented them taking place; both arms were not yet in a position to begin raiding, as they lacked suitable bases and had few airships to deploy.

Behncke continued lobbying, and produced a document focusing on an article of the second Hague Convention of 1907 that stated that military establishments, located within undefended areas, could be attacked. He argued that, since London contained military installations in the form of its docks, factories and anti-aircraft guns, it was a legitimate target. Behncke was not alone in his desire to bomb London and, under increasing pressure, the Kaiser finally accepted the reality of a limited bombing campaign on England in January 1915. However, on the Kaiser's insistence, London was excluded. Undeterred, Behncke produced a list of recommended targets that included the Admiralty buildings, Woolwich Arsenal, the Bank of England and the Stock Exchange. In February, the Kaiser accepted the addition of the London docks as a legitimate target, but still clung naively to the notion that he could specifically forbid attacks on residential areas, royal palaces and important monuments. Yet the combination of unsophisticated bombing methods and the proximity of countless tightly packed streets around the docks meant the restrictions were impossible to observe. Then, in May 1915, the Kaiser approved bombing east of the Tower of London, followed in July by the inclusion of the whole of London. Behncke had finally achieved his wish.

Konteradmiral Paul Behncke, Reichskriegsmarine (1866–1937). As Deputy Chief of the Naval Staff he was one of the most persistent campaigners in persuading the Kaiser to approve aerial bombing raids on London. He highlighted the importance of London as a target and in particular the Admiralty buildings in Whitehall as well as the docks. He confidently expected these raids 'to cause panic in the population, which may possibly render it doubtful that the war can be continued'. (C. Ablett)

Fregattenkapitän Peter Strasser

Strasser joined the German Navy as a 15-year-old, before entering the naval academy at Kiel. He made good progress through the ranks, serving on a number of ships between 1897 and 1902, during which time he became expert in naval gunnery. After this period at sea, Strasser joined the Navy Office as a gunnery specialist, but in 1911 he volunteered for aviation training. Two years later, in September 1913, Kvtkpt Strasser was offered command of the Naval Airship Division.

Strasser, displaying his inspirational leadership qualities to the full, quickly galvanized the moribund division and instilled fresh confidence and pride into his men. He then made his mark on the naval hierarchy, pushing his ideas for the development of the Airship Division all the way to the top at a time when some were considering disbanding the division altogether, eventually earning promotion to Fregattenkapitän. Although a harsh disciplinarian, Strasser also took great care of his men, and those that passed through his rigorous training schedule developed a fine *esprit de corps* and hero-worship for their commander. Despite numerous setbacks during the war, Strasser never lost his unswerving faith in the Zeppelin, although Vizeadmiral Reinhard Scheer reined in his aggressive independence a little following his appointment as Commander-in Chief of the High Seas Fleet in January 1916. However, Strasser's devotion to the Airship Division received recognition in November 1916 with his appointment as Führer der Luftschiffe, carrying the equivalent rank of Admiral second class.

Fregattenkapitän Peter Strasser, Reichskriegsmarine (1876–1918). Strasser took command of the Naval Airship Division in September 1913 following the death of its commander, Kvtkpt Friedrich Metzing, in the crash of Zeppelin *L.2*. An inspirational and charismatic leader, he regularly flew on missions to understand first hand the difficulties his crews experienced, although many considered him a 'Jonah' as those airships often returned early with mechanical problems. In spite of mounting Zeppelin losses, he maintained an unshaken belief in the value of airships right to the end.

OPPOSING PLANS

The development of airships opened the path for a new branch of warfare: strategic bombing. With aviation still a new science, there were no established rules or tactics for aerial conflict. As such, the aviators of both Britain and Germany constantly evolved, rapidly devising and implementing new strategies and tactics in response to changing circumstances.

British strategy and tactics

At the outbreak of war, the Royal Flying Corps mustered five squadrons, of which four were active and had departed for France with the BEF. No.1 Squadron, formerly assigned to airships, remained behind at Brooklands in Surrey, to be re-equipped with aeroplanes. On paper, the RFC claimed about 190 aircraft, but many of these were unfit for service. The four squadrons that went to France took 63 aircraft of various types; of those left in Britain, perhaps as few as 20 were fit for service.

The RNAS established a number of air stations along the coast, mainly between the Humber and the Thames, where it based its 39 aeroplanes, 52 seaplanes and a flying boat – but perhaps only half of these were operational. Amongst its eclectic collection the RNAS included one Vickers F.B.4 'Gunbus', the only fighter aircraft in Britain at that time, mounting a single machine gun in the observer's cockpit. In August 1914, as part of its commitment to the defence of London, the RNAS took over Hendon airfield in north-west London.

On 5 September 1914 Churchill outlined his home defence plan. He announced that the front line – formed by the RNAS in France – would engage enemy airships close to their own bases, attack those bases and establish aerial control over a wide area extending from Dunkirk. An aerial strike force formed the second line, located 'at some convenient point within a range of a line drawn from Dover to London, with local defence flights at Eastchurch [Isle of Sheppey] and Calshot [Southampton Water]'. Other aircraft with an interceptor role occupied stations along the east coast. The RNAS pilots based at Hendon formed the final line in the airborne defence plan.

Other defensive moves saw additional anti-aircraft guns assigned to key military installations, while instructions for the implementation of a blackout came into effect on 1 October. Amongst other requirements, black paint applied to the tops of street lamps dimmed their light and notices instructed the public to make sure they had well-fitting curtains.

The following month, October 1914, the RNAS requested RFC assistance in defending London. In response, four aircraft from No. 1 Squadron were dispatched, two to Hounslow and two to Joyce Green (near Dartford). By the end of the year the Admiralty defence plan had formalized and about 40 RNAS aircraft based at 12 stations covered the approaches to Britain's east coast between Killingholme (near Grimsby) in the north and Dover in the south. In addition, over 20 seaplanes remained on stand-by.

This system provided a two-tier defence. It took a long time for an aircraft to climb to a height where it could engage an enemy airship. This plan anticipated that those aircraft based inland would receive enough warning of a raid on London to ascend to meet it, while in the meantime those on the coast would attain the altitude needed to intercept the raiders on their return journey.

Aircraft production increased rapidly to meet the demand from both the RFC and RNAS, and by the end of 1914 they had together ordered almost a thousand new aeroplanes. The Royal Aircraft Factory at Farnborough had been working on producing a stable and easy to fly machine for reconnaissance and scouting duties. This resulted in the B.E. (Blériot Experimental) series, of which the government approved the production of the BE2c variant in great quantities. However, when fast and nimble German fighters began to appear on the Western Front, the slow and steady BE2c became an easy victim. Back in England, and relegated to home defence duties, these very same qualities, combined with new developments in armaments, eventually saw the BE2c develop into an excellent night-flying anti-Zeppelin platform.

Although London could now, on paper at least, boast an aerial defence force, in reality it offered little opposition to raiding airships. The British understood that the use of highly inflammable hydrogen as a lifting gas, contained in a number of separate gas cells within the rigid framework, presented a great weakness in airship design, but struggled for a means to exploit this. Ordinary bullets carried little threat, merely puncturing individual gas cells with only a limited immediate effect on overall performance. Therefore, at the beginning of the war, many pilots flew into action armed with single-shot, breech-loading Martini-Henry cavalry

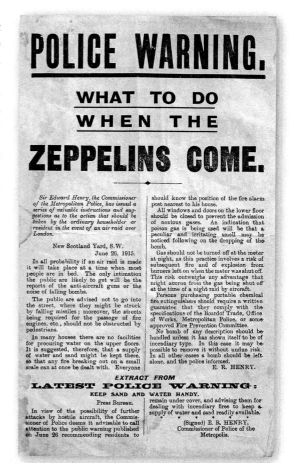

This folded leaflet, distributed with the *Daily News*, offers simple advice for householders to employ during an air raid. Inside the leaflet, the *Daily News* offers readers free 'Zeppelin Bombardment Insurance' – for those who subscribe to the newspaper.

Blériot Experimental 2c (BE2c), in situ at the Imperial War Museum, Lambeth. The Royal Aircraft Factory designed BE2c carried a single 90 hp engine, had a wing span of 36ft 10in. and was 27ft 3in. in length. Outclassed on the front line in France, it proved an ideal anti-Zeppelin night-fighter.

The DELAG airship *Hansa* began operating as a civil craft in July 1912, but in August 1914, having completed 399 flights, she was handed over to the government as a training ship.

carbines, of Zulu War vintage, firing a new 'flaming bullet'. This .45-calibre bullet contained an incendiary compound, but pilots struggled to hold their aircraft steady while using both hands to fire the carbine.

A number of bombs were available for use against airships. The main problem with these was that the pilot needed to coax his aircraft up above the hostile airship to drop them, and yet the available aircraft did not have the ability to out-climb the airships. The aerial armoury included the 20 lb explosive Hales bomb and 10 lb and 20 lb incendiary bombs. Another weapon in this early arsenal was the fearsome sounding 'Fiery Grapnel'. This device comprised a four-pointed hook, loaded with explosives, that was trailed on a cable below the aircraft until, hopefully, it caught on the outer skin of an airship and detonated.

To boost the initial provision of guns in Whitehall, London received a further ten weapons detailed to serve in an anti-aircraft role, but all generally lacked the elevation or range to hit airships. Special constables, enrolled in the Royal Naval Volunteer Reserve, manned these four 6-pdr Hotchkiss guns and six 1-pdr pom-poms, but the Hotchkiss struggled with an effective anti-aircraft range of about 3,600ft while the pom-poms were short of even that, both well below the operational height of a Zeppelin. In addition, the Royal Marines manned two 3in. naval guns in the capital, one at Tower Bridge, and the other in Regent's Park. Behind this flimsy defensive façade, London lay open and exposed to attack.

German plans

At the outbreak of war the German Army had 10 operational airships (nine Zeppelins and one Schütte-Lanz), although this figure included three commercial DELAG Zeppelins acquired for training purposes. The army assigned four airships to the Western Front and three to the east. The navy had just one airship, *L.3*, which came into service at the end of May 1914. The army, tactically naive when it came to the deployment of their airships, initially used them in a low-level, infantry support role and within three

German army and navy airship bases

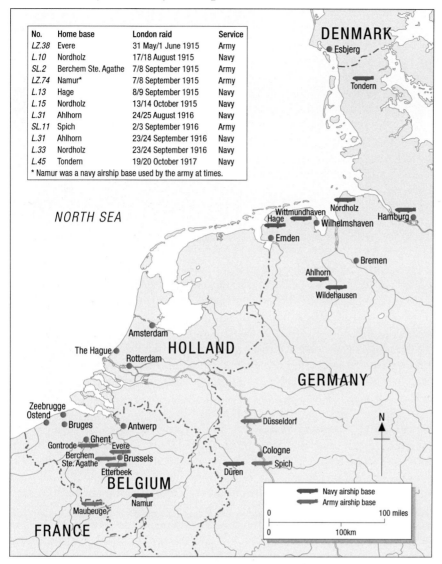

No.	Home base	London raid	Service
LZ.38	Evere	31 May/1 June 1915	Army
L.10	Nordholz	17/18 August 1915	Navy
SL.2	Berchem Ste. Agathe	7/8 September 1915	Army
LZ.74	Namur*	7/8 September 1915	Army
L.13	Hage	8/9 September 1915	Navy
L.15	Nordholz	13/14 October 1915	Navy
L.31	Ahlhorn	24/25 August 1916	Navy
SL.11	Spich	2/3 September 1916	Army
L.31	Ahlhorn	23/24 September 1916	Navy
L.33	Nordholz	23/24 September 1916	Navy
L.45	Tondern	19/20 October 1917	Navy

* Namur was a navy airship base used by the army at times.

weeks of the start of the war had lost three of those in the west. Before the month was out they had also lost one at the Battle of Tannenberg in the east. Just two Zeppelins and one Schütte-Lanz remained operational, along with the navy's single airship, and with that detailed for naval patrol work there was, as yet, no threat to Britain from the air.

New airships, ordered before the war, gradually began to arrive and by the end of August 1914 the navy doubled its strength with the acquisition of *L.4*. This was the first of ten M-class airships, evenly distributed between the army and navy, based on the same design as the pre-war *L.3*. The order reached completion in February 1915.

With more airships on the production line, the requirement now was for sheds in which to house them. Early in 1913 the navy selected a remote spot at Nordholz, near Cuxhaven, to build an airship base, complete with four revolving sheds; this provision would enable take-off whatever the wind direction. While Nordholz was prepared, the navy rented a hangar at

Fuhlsbüttel, near Hamburg. The army initially based their airships in Belgium for service in the west but later relocated to Germany.

With increasing demands from the armed services, the Zeppelin Company proposed to produce a bigger airship by adapting a commercial design they had been working on. This design introduced duralumin (an aluminium alloy) to replace aluminium, which made the framework even lighter without a reduction in strength. This model, the P-class, with a hull of 531ft would be 18ft longer than the *L.3* design and, with a 60ft diameter, would be 12ft wider. This additional size increased the gas capacity from 880,000 to 1,126,000 cubic feet. The effect of the greater capacity was to increase the unloaded ceiling of the new Zeppelins from about 8,000 to 10,000ft. Adding a fourth engine increased speed from 52 to 63 mph. The new design also increased crew safety and comfort by providing fully enclosed gondolas (the cars suspended from the hull) for the first time. The armed services readily accepted the new design and ordered 22, while plans to build new sheds went ahead too, the navy expecting those at Tondern and Hage to be ready by the end of the year. Both services also placed new orders with Schütte-Lanz.

The army took delivery of *LZ.38*, the first of the eagerly awaited P-class Zeppelins, on 3 April 1915. The navy waited another five weeks for their first vessel, the *L.10*, and the order was complete by the end of 1915. The first of the navy's new sheds at Nordholz opened in late January 1915, at Tondern in late March and at Hage in April.

Yet while the army and navy awaited delivery of their new airships, Kaiser Wilhelm firmly blocked any attempt to bomb England, despite the determined efforts of men like the Deputy Chief of the Naval Staff, Konteradmiral Paul Behncke, backed by Kvtkpt Peter Strasser.

While the German airship commanders strained at the leash to bomb England, and prevented from doing so by Kaiser Wilhelm, British airmen experienced no such restrictions. Heeding Churchill's directive that the defence of Britain started at the airship bases in Europe, the RNAS launched a successful raid on the army airship shed at Düsseldorf on 8 October 1914, incinerating Zeppelin *Z.IX*. Another raid, on 21 November, daringly targeted Friedrichshafen, the home of the Zeppelin Company, and caused much damage, although it narrowly missed destroying the navy's new *L.7* as it approached completion. Then, on Christmas Day 1914, the British attempted an ambitious combined air and sea operation, with seaplanes attacking the nearly completed Nordholz sheds. The raid failed and was to be the last of its kind, but the Germans were not aware of this. The German navy, concerned that these raids would destroy the airships before they had even begun to attack England, increased the pressure on Kaiser Wilhelm to sanction air attacks. Finally, on 9 January 1915, he gave his qualified approval. There were to be no attacks on London, but the Thames estuary and east coast of Britain were now legitimate targets.

The revolving shed at Nordholz was originally 597ft long and designed to hold two airships. As larger airships were ordered, the angular extensions were added to increase the length to 656ft. One officer described Nordholz as 'the most God-forsaken hole on earth.'

THE 1915 RAIDS

THE CAMPAIGN BEGINS

The Kaiser's approval immediately spurred the German Naval Airship Division into action, with Strasser ordering four of his airships to attack England on 13 January 1915. However, bad weather forced the abandonment of the raid. The weather was probably Britain's greatest ally in restricting German determination to bomb the nation into submission. Heavy rain absorbed by the outer envelope of an airship added tons of extra weight, as did snow and ice, forcing them dangerously low. When ice froze on the propellers, sharp fragments flung backwards with terrific force could puncture the outer envelope and internal gas cells. Thunder, lightning and fog each offered their own dangers. Strong headwinds could bring progress to a halt, while crosswinds could blow an airship miles off course. Navigation itself was basic, with each airship carrying a magnetic compass and steering by dead reckoning over the sea. This process used a combination of speed and compass direction to calculate a position, but the direction and speed of the wind greatly affected accuracy. Over land, crews used maps to identify ground features and towns, often illuminating them with magnesium-burning parachute flares. However, if the wind pushed the ship off course then landfall over England was easy to misjudge, adding confusion to later aerial identification of targets. From April

The open control gondola of an M-class Zeppelin. Airship crews only benefited from enclosed gondolas with the introduction of later models. The square panel to the rear of the control gondola in this picture is an engine radiator. (C. Ablett)

Army Zeppelin *LZ.38*, the first P-class to enter service. *LZ.38* was 536ft long and was powered by three 210 hp Maybach engines (later P-class vessels had four engines). Commanded by Hptmn Erich Linnarz, she was the first airship to bomb London.

1915 airship commanders benefited from the use of radio bearings to pinpoint their position, but the accuracy often left much to be desired. At the same time British stations were able to intercept and plot these transmissions too, forcing airship commanders to keep communication to a minimum. There was also the constant threat of mechanical breakdown. After surmounting all these dangers, there remained one more obstacle to overcome, namely the aeroplanes and anti-aircraft guns of Britain's Home Defence organization. Initially, though, this opposition was limited.

After the first aborted mission, Strasser ordered a second six days later, on the night of 19/20 January 1915. This time two navy M-class Zeppelins, *L.3* and *L.4*, successfully crossed the North Sea, but were blown off course from their intended target of the Humber. Instead, unopposed by the RNAS and RFC, they released their bombs over Great Yarmouth, Snettisham and King's Lynn in Norfolk. Konteradmiral Paul Behncke received the news of this first successful Zeppelin raid with great delight, enthusiastically shared by the German population. Back in England, shocked families mourned the deaths of four innocent civilians while 16 others received treatment for their injuries.

On 12 February, in the face of constant pressure, the Kaiser relented and declared the London docks a permitted target. Two weeks later navy Zeppelin *L.8* flew from Düsseldorf to attack London but strong headwinds made the attack impossible. She sought refuge at Gontrode army airship base near Ghent in Belgium, but then, on her return journey, a combination of small-arms fire and engine failure forced her down and strong winds destroyed her on the ground.

The Army Airship Service launched its four available airships against England on 17 March, but heavy fog over the English Channel forced them back. Returning to base, one airship suffered damage on landing and three days later, while attacking Paris, enemy fire forced down another. Then, on 13 April, anti-aircraft fire brought down a third vessel, *LZ.35*, near Ypres. Fortunately for the army they took delivery of the last of their M-class airships – *LZ.37* – in March and the first of their P-class airships – *LZ.38* and *LZ.39* – in April 1915.

With the army licking its wounds, the onus returned to Strasser and the Naval Airship Division. On 14 April Kptlt Heinrich Mathy in *L.9* bombed around Blyth and Wallsend in the north-east of England, but the damage was negligible. One British aircraft took off from RNAS Whitley Bay and patrolled over Newcastle but, with no searchlights in operation, *L.9* escaped undetected.

The following day three airships – *L.5*, *L.6* and *L.7* – set out to raid the Humber, but strong winds again blew them off course. *L.5* and *L.6* released bombs over Suffolk and Essex before returning to base.

Strasser came to the conclusion that his older M-class Zeppelins, with their limited endurance and lifting capabilities, were not up to the task of attacking England, and put further plans on hold until his new P-class airships were ready. Now the pendulum swung back to the Army Airship Service, and in particular to Hptmn Erich Linnarz.

Linnarz, appointed to command the first of the new Zeppelins, began very careful planning, for the general feeling amongst airship crews was that the Kaiser would soon have to declare London open to airship attack. On 29 April Linnarz bombed Ipswich and Bury St. Edmunds from *LZ.38*; thick coastal mist prevented RNAS Yarmouth from opposing the raid. Linnarz returned on the night of 9/10 May. This time he made two successful bombing runs over Southend on the south coast of Essex. *LZ.38* continued its probing raids and on the night of 16/17 May, dropped bombs on Ramsgate and Dover in Kent. For the first time a searchlight illuminated a Zeppelin raid and a defence pilot – Flight Sub-Lt Redford Mulock, RNAS – actually saw a Zeppelin, although *LZ.38* easily out-climbed him. Linnarz bombed Southend again on the night of 26/27 May, but with little advance warning, the five RNAS aircraft that took off were unable to climb high enough before *LZ.38* turned for home. The sum total of material damage accumulated on these four raids only amounted to about £17,000, but they claimed the lives of six civilians and caused injuries to a similar number. Although not destruction on a grand scale, it proved valuable experience for Linnarz and the crew of *LZ.38*, experience they were about to put to devastating effect.

THE FIRST LONDON RAID – THE ARMY CLAIMS THE PRIZE

In May 1915 the Kaiser, under constant pressure, gave his reluctant approval for the bombing of the British capital east of a line parallel with the Tower of London. Overlooking a number of stipulations imposed by the Kaiser, the Army Airship Service prepared to lead the way.

At about dusk on the evening of Monday 31 May, Linnarz ascended in *LZ.38* from the base at Evere, just north of Brussels, while *LZ.37* took off from Namur. Damage to the outer envelope forced *LZ.37* to return early, but, unhindered, Linnarz flew over Margate at 21.42 and headed for the now familiar landmark of Southend. From there he steered a westerly course for the capital.

It was now almost 10 months since Britain had declared war on Germany. The feared Zeppelin onslaught on London had not materialized and the tentative probes at East Anglia, Essex and Kent had little effect on Londoners. Although the streets remained darkened, most people went about their lives as normal. The Metropolitan Police received notification of an impending raid at about 22.55. While they were still absorbing this unexpected news, a

The first house in London to be bombed: 16 Alkham Road, in Stoke Newington.

shocked sub-inspector of the Special Constabulary observed a Zeppelin approaching Stoke Newington Station. Moments later bombs began to fall.

The first bomb on London, an incendiary, fell just south of the railway station on a house at 16 Alkham Road, the home of a clerk, Albert Lovell. It smashed through the roof, setting fire to the bedroom and back room on the top floor. The bewildered Mr Lovell, his wife, children and two guests tumbled from the house without injury and the fire brigade arrived promptly to extinguish the blaze. Linnarz passed on over Stoke Newington High Street before turning onto a course heading south, directly on a line leading towards the Tower of London and parallel with Stoke Newington Road/Kingsland Road in the direction of Hoxton. In Cowper Road, a Mr C. Smith was in bed when he heard 'a terrible rushing of wind and a shout of "Fire" and "The Germans are here."' He rushed his children down to the basement, then went outside to find the neighbouring house on fire. An incendiary bomb had crashed through the roof; passing through the top floor it set fire to a second floor bedroom where Samuel Leggatt's five children were sleeping. Leggatt fought his way into the room, suffering burns to his face and hands, but, helped by neighbours, pulled four of his children to safety and led them away to hospital. Tragically, in the confusion, the family believed neighbours had taken in the youngest child, three-year-old Elsie, but later a policeman discovered her burnt body under the bed where she had crawled to hide.

Linnarz, in *LZ.38*, continued flying south, deploying a heavy concentration of bombs as he went. Two incendiaries fell on 187 Balls Pond Road, a three-storied house owned by a builder, Thomas Sharpling. A police constable who saw the bombs fall said that he 'heard the sound of machinery in the air, and suddenly the house burst into flames.' Sharpling and his family scrambled clear while a lodger leapt from a window into a blanket, but later searchers discovered the charred bodies of two other lodgers kneeling by their bed as if in prayer: Henry Good, a 49-year-old labourer, and his wife Caroline.

Other incendiary bombs fell relatively harmlessly in Southgate Road, yet they provided a rude awakening for the residents. One of them, Mr A.B. Cook, later recalled that people were unaware what was happening at first: 'People flung up their windows and saw an astonishing sight, the roadway a mass of flames... Flames reached a height of 20ft... The sky was red with the light of flames.'

LZ.38 continued wreaking destruction through the streets of Hoxton and continued over Shoreditch High Street. Here, at 23.08, three incendiaries fell on the roof of the Shoreditch Empire music hall, where a late performance was in progress. The manager calmly addressed the audience who then left in an orderly manner as the band 'played lively airs'. Further along the High Street bombs fell on Bishopsgate Goods Station, then, within a mile of the Tower of London, Linnarz turned away to the south-east and bombed Spitalfields. Crossing the Whitechapel Road and then heading east over

Commercial Road, bombs hit a whisky distillery and a synagogue, before two explosive bombs fell in the roadway in Christian Street; 12 passers-by received injuries and one, an eight-year-old boy called Samuel Reuben, who was on his way home from the cinema, died. One of the badly injured, Lily Leahman, died two days later. These bombs fell only 600 yards from the London Western Dock.

Large crowds gathered in the streets throughout the bombed area but the police reported that the behaviour was generally good and no panic ensued. However, there was an incident where a mob attacked a Russian nightwatchman as he left the burning premises of a bamboo furniture manufacturer in Hoxton Street, believing him to be German and the cause of the fire. Tension simmered the following day (1 June), and anti-German feeling ran high in Shoreditch where mobs attacked and damaged a number of shops owned by persons believed to be of German nationality.

Linnarz turned north-east and, passing over Stepney, dropped four explosive and two incendiary bombs, which caused only minor damage. Almost three miles further on he dropped an incendiary over Stratford at about 23.30, that smashed through the roof of 26 Colgrave Road, passing through the bedroom of Peter Gillies and his wife, within five feet of where they lay in bed. A neighbour who saw the bomb fall said, 'I heard the droning of an aeroplane but I could not see anything. According to the noise it came lower and then I saw the bomb drop. It was simply a dark object and I saw it drop through the roof of number 26.' Then, half a mile further on, *LZ.38* dropped five bombs over Leytonstone, causing minor damage before heading back towards Southend and out over the coast near Foulness.

A typical German incendiary bomb. The interior was packed with a mixture of Benzol, tar and Thermite, which burned at an extremely high temperature, easily setting wood and combustible materials on fire. The outside of the bomb was covered with tarred rope. (Shuttleworth Collection)

The main bombing run, from Stoke Newington to Stepney, lasted 20 minutes. The Fire Brigade attended 41 fires; members of the public extinguished others. Seven premises were completely burnt out, but the largest fire occurred at 31 Ivy Street, Hoxton, gutting a cabinetmaker's and timber yard. The Fire Brigade calculated material damage for the night at £18,596, with seven killed. Some 3,000 lb of bombs were dropped (the police recorded 91 incendiary and 28 explosive bombs and two grenades).

The night of 31 May was dark, with no moon, and, although the atmosphere remained fairly clear, no searchlights located *LZ.38* and no guns opened fire, and hardly anyone actually saw her as she passed over the capital. The RNAS managed to get 15 aircraft airborne, but only one pilot, flying from Rochford near Southend, saw *LZ.38*. Engine trouble forced him down before he could climb high enough to engage.

There could be no hiding the fact: a Zeppelin had passed freely over London and, facing no opposition, had bombed civilian targets at will before departing without a shot fired in return. The German government in Berlin falsely claimed that the raid 'threw numerous bombs on the wharves and docks of London.' In Britain, the government slapped an immediate press restriction on reporting airship raids, limiting coverage to official communications.

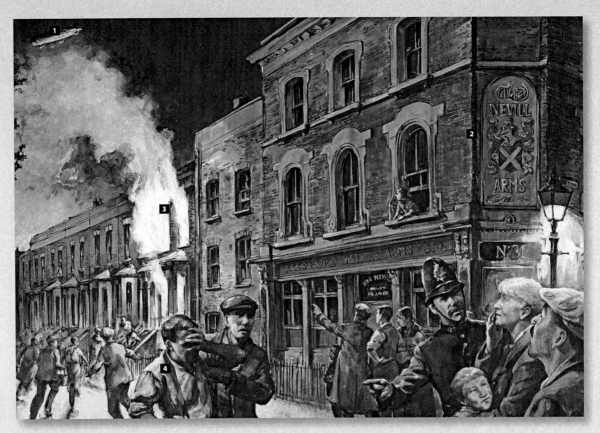

LONDON'S FIRST ZEPPELIN RAID – NEVILLE ROAD, STOKE NEWINGTON (pp. 22–23)

Shortly after 23.00 on Monday 31 May 1915, Zeppelin *LZ.38* **(1)** appeared unannounced over Stoke Newington in north London. The commander, Erich Linnarz, later described the tense moment as he prepared to release the first bombs on the capital:

'My finger hovered on the button that electrically operated the bombing apparatus. Then I pressed it. We waited. Minutes seemed to pass before, above the humming song of the engines, there rose a shattering roar… A cascade of orange sparks shot upwards, and a billow of incandescent smoke drifted slowly away to reveal a red gash of raging fire on the face of the wounded city.'

The first bomb fell on Alkham Road, the next in Dynevor Road. *LZ.38* then steered over Neville Road. An incendiary bomb crashed through the roof of an outbuilding at the back of the Neville Arms **(2)**, but failed to ignite. Two houses further on, at No. 27 **(3)**, another incendiary smashed through the roof causing a tremendous conflagration. Five rooms were gutted and two badly damaged. Alfred West, the 26-year-old son of the owner, suffered burns to his face **(4)**. The fire was eventually extinguished by the police and neighbours as *LZ.38* continued on its path of destruction.

FIRST BLOOD

The German Army Airship Service took the laurels for the first successful raid on London, a fact not well received by the Navy Airship Division. The navy now prepared to send its first P-class Zeppelin, *L.10*, into action against Britain. On the afternoon of 4 June, *L.10* and the Schütte-Lanz airship *SL.3* set off, but only *L.10* headed for London. The commander of *L.10*, Kptlt Klaus Hirsch, misjudged his position and, believing he could not reach the city, instead bombed what he thought was the naval base at Harwich. Hirsch in fact had been carried south-west by strong winds and his bombs actually fell on Gravesend, within easy reach of the city. Fog hampered British defensive sorties that night and neither *L.10* nor *SL.3*, which sought targets in the north of England, encountered any opposition.

Two days later, on the night of 6/7 June, another raid took place, and for the first time both the navy and army sent airships out on the same night. The navy sent Kptlt Mathy in *L.9* to 'attack London if possible, otherwise a coastal town according to choice'. Weather conditions forced Mathy to switch his target to Hull, where his bombs caused widespread devastation and claimed many lives.

The army raid that night comprised three Zeppelins – *LZ.37*, *LZ.38* and *LZ.39* – and resulted in a fresh disaster for the Army Airship Service. Hauptmann Linnarz knew the route to London well now, but *LZ.38* developed engine trouble early in the flight, forcing him to return to his base at Evere. Meanwhile, *LZ.37* and *LZ.39* ran into thick fog over the North Sea and abandoned the raid too. As they returned, a flight of four aircraft of No.1 (RNAS) Squadron, based at Furnes in France, was preparing to raid the Belgian airship sheds. Linnarz had already docked *LZ.38* when two Henry Farman aircraft arrived over Evere. Their bombs destroyed the shed and with it *LZ.38*, only six days after it had successfully bombed London. Meanwhile, one of the other pilots, Flight Sub-Lt R.A.J. Warneford, flying a Morane-Saulnier Parasol, caught sight of *LZ.37* returning to the shed at Gontrode and turned in pursuit. Her commander, Oberleutnant van der Haegen, made a dash for his base, attempting to keep his assailant at bay with machine-gun fire. As *LZ.37* descended, Warneford climbed above her and released six bombs over the doomed airship. *LZ.37* exploded into a mass of burning flame and crashed down to earth into the St Amansdsberg convent school, injuring two nuns and killing a third. Miraculously, one of her crew survived. After an eventful return journey Warneford became an instant hero, an antidote to the growing anger in Britain caused by the inability of the home defences to engage the Zeppelin raiders. He immediately received the award of the Victoria Cross, but did not live long to enjoy his success; ten days after his exploits he was killed when his plane crashed en route for Paris.

The vulnerability of the Belgian hangars now became apparent and outweighed the benefit they offered of a shorter route to England. Both the army and navy abandoned any further plans for their regular use.

The navy returned to the offensive on the night of 15/16 June. Two P-class Zeppelins, *L.10* and *L.11*, left Nordholz and headed for Tyneside, but only *L.10* reached the target. On his return the commander of *L.10*, Kptlt. Klaus Hirsch, reported to Strasser that the evening had never really become dark, pointing out that the June and July nights were too short to provide effective cover for air attacks. Strasser agreed with Hirsch and the initial flurry of raiding by the naval airships ended. The army, meanwhile,

The 31 May/1 June 1915 raid on London: *LZ.38* (Hptmn Erich Linnarz)

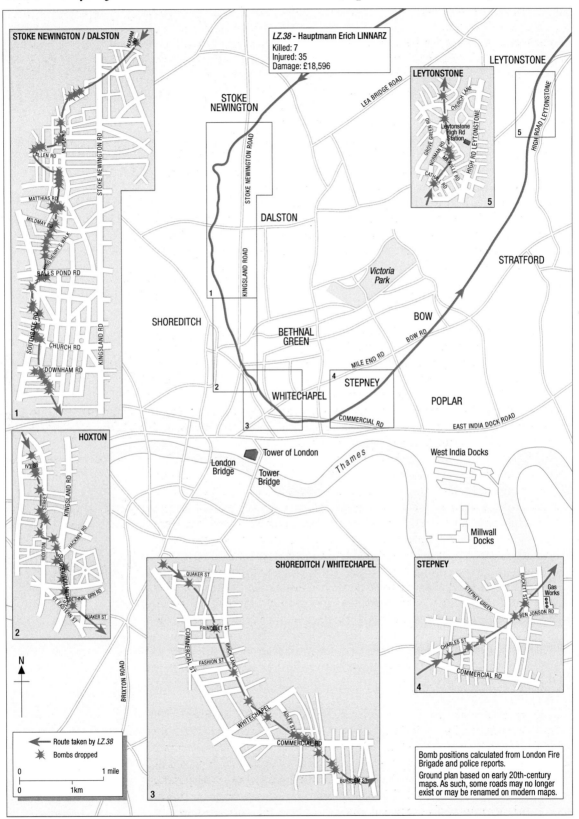

STOKE NEWINGTON / DALSTON

LZ.38 - Hauptmann Erich LINNARZ
Killed: 7
Injured: 35
Damage: £18,596

LEYTONSTONE

LEYTONSTONE

STOKE NEWINGTON

LEA BRIDGE ROAD

Leytonstone High Rd Station

CHURCH LANE

GROVE GREEN RD

NORMAN RD

MANVILLE RD

HIGH RD LEYTONSTONE

CATHALL RD

HIGH ROAD LEYTONSTONE

5

DALSTON

STOKE NEWINGTON ROAD

KINGSLAND ROAD

Victoria Park

STRATFORD

SHOREDITCH

BETHNAL GREEN

BOW

BOW RD

MILE END RD

STEPNEY

WHITECHAPEL

POPLAR

COMMERCIAL RD

EAST INDIA DOCK ROAD

ALUM RD

NEWLAND

ALLEN RD

MATTHIAS RD

MILDMAY RD

KING HENRY'S WALK

BALLS POND RD

SOUTHGATE RD

CHURCH RD

KINGSLAND RD

DOWNHAM RD

1

Tower of London

London Bridge

Tower Bridge

Thames

West India Docks

Millwall Docks

HOXTON

IVY ST

STREET

KINGSLAND RD

HOXTON

SHOREDITCH HIGH ST

HACKNEY RD

BETHNAL GRN RD

GT EASTERN ST

QUAKER ST

2

SHOREDITCH / WHITECHAPEL

QUAKER ST

PRINCELET ST

COMMERCIAL ST

BRICK LANE

FASHION ST

WHITECHAPEL

ADLER ST

COMMERCIAL RD

BURSLEM ST

3

STEPNEY

STEPNEY GREEN

DUCKETT ST

Gas Works

BEN JONSON RD

CHARLES ST

COMMERCIAL RD

4

N

BRIXTON ROAD

⟵ Route taken by *LZ.38*
✴ Bombs dropped

0 ———————————— 1 mile
0 ———————————— 1km

Bomb positions calculated from London Fire Brigade and police reports.

Ground plan based on early 20th-century maps. As such, some roads may no longer exist or may be renamed on modern maps.

with its last two operational airships (*Z.XII* and *LZ.39*) dispatched to the eastern front, temporarily had no offensive capability.

The success of Warneford in bringing down *LZ.37* with bombs confirmed for many in authority that this remained the most likely method of destroying airships. A theory much in evidence suggested that a layer of inert gas surrounded the hydrogen cells contained within the outer envelope, preventing their ignition by incendiary bullets. As such, the belief became prevalent that an airship could only be destroyed by a major trauma caused by an explosive bomb – a theory seemingly confirmed by Warneford's singular success. In fact, 10 days before the destruction of *LZ.37*, the War Office informed the RFC that it believed the 'flaming bullets' were 'useless against Zeppelins'. However, incendiary bullets were the answer, but it was not until 1916 that the authorities finally recognized this.

In Britain the uneasy relationship between the War Office and Admiralty as to the responsibility for Home Defence continued. When Arthur Balfour replaced Churchill as First Lord of the Admiralty in May 1915, just before the first London raid, he felt the defence of London was not a naval responsibility. In June, the Admiralty requested that the War Office take on the role and, after some posturing, the War Office finally stated that they hoped to be able to fulfil the obligations for home defence by January 1916.

In June 1915 the RFC had 20 aeroplanes detailed to support the RNAS in the defence of London. These flew from Brooklands, Farnborough, Dover, Hounslow, Joyce Green, Northolt, Shoreham and Gosport. All 20 carried an armament of bombs, except two Vickers Gunbuses based at Joyce Green that mounted machine guns and two BE2c aircraft at Dover fitted with the Fiery Grapnel. Unfortunately, nine aircraft were the unsuitable Martinsyde S1 Scout, unsteady in the air, with a low ceiling and sluggish climbing ability.

Despite this necessary co-operation, relations between the War Office and the Admiralty were not always harmonious, and, against this lack of a unified defence, the Zeppelins returned in August 1915 after a two-month absence. By this time the Kaiser had relented under pressure and approved unrestricted bombing of London.

Flight Sub-Lieutenant Reginald Warneford, RNAS, at Hendon in February 1915. He was awarded the Victoria Cross after becoming the first pilot to destroy a Zeppelin in the air when he brought down *LZ.37* on 7 June 1915. He died ten days later when his aircraft crashed in France.

THE SECOND LONDON RAID – THE NAVY STRIKES

Fresh from operations with the fleet, the Naval Airship Division resumed its air campaign against Britain on the night of 9/10 August and, despite launching four P-class Zeppelins – *L.10*, *L.11*, *L.12* and *L.13* – against London, none reached the target. Oberleutnant-zur-See Werner Peterson in *L.12* caused minor damage in Dover, but, illuminated by a searchlight, he came under anti-aircraft fire. With two gas cells punctured, *L.12* began to lose height. Limping homewards, Peterson ordered all excess weight overboard to lighten his ship, but she came down in the sea off Zeebrugge. A torpedo boat towed her into Ostend where, with no repair facilities available, Peterson reluctantly had her dismantled.

Undeterred and making the most of the dark skies of the new moon, Strasser authorized another raid on London three days later, on the night of 12/13 August. Zeppelin *L.9* joined the three survivors of the previous raid, but a combination of strong headwinds and engine problems prevented any of them reaching the city. Only *L.10* reached England, where it bombed Harwich, but four aircraft that ascended from RNAS Yarmouth failed to intercept her.

Eleven weeks had now passed since the Army Airship Service had successfully bombed London, and Strasser was unceasing in his determination to strike an equal blow for the navy. He launched his next raid on the dark and moonless night of 17/18 August, sending *L.10*, *L.11*, *L.13* and *L.14* against the capital. The frustrated Kptlt Mathy in *L.13* turned for home early again with engine trouble, the third time in three raids for the new airship. Kptlt Alois Böcker, commanding *L.14*, also returned with engine problems. Further south *L.11*, commanded by Oblt-z-S Horst von Buttlar, flew across Kent, dropping bombs at Ashford and on villages near Faversham before setting course for home, although his report falsely claimed great success in bombing Woolwich, some 40 miles from Ashford. Elsewhere, however, Strasser could take comfort, for finally a navy Zeppelin had reached London.

Oberleutnant-zur-See Friedrich Wenke brought *L.10* in over the coast about six miles north of Felixstowe at around 21.00. Steering southwards, he skirted Felixstowe, avoided Harwich, and followed the River Stour to Manningtree in Essex. From there he steered by the railway line to Colchester and passed over Witham at about 21.50, before skirting the north of Chelmsford at Broomfield. From there *L.10* headed west towards Waltham Abbey. The two RNAS aircraft at Chelmsford did not get airborne until 45 minutes after *L.10* had passed, but over Waltham Abbey a searchlight caught the airship and the anti-aircraft gun stationed there managed to fire off two rounds before *L.10* moved out of range and headed for London. Wenke later

The stricken *L.12* being towed back to Ostend. The RNAS sent up eight pilots in an attempt to bomb the wreck, but, encountering heavy anti-aircraft fire, all were unsuccessful and one, Flight Lt D.K. Johnston, was killed.

Zeppelin *L.10*, the first of the Naval Airship Division airships to bomb London. *L.10* entered service in May 1915, based at Nordholz. She participated in five raids on England before lightning destroyed her on 3 September 1915. (Luftschiffbau Zeppelin)

BELOW, LEFT
Friedrich Wenke reported that *L.10*'s initial bombs fell between Blackfriars and London Bridge, as recorded in this illustration that appeared in a German newspaper. Wenke was wrong: his bombs fell near the great reservoirs in the Lea Valley

reported that the London searchlights found it very difficult to hold him in their beams at his height of 10,200ft (almost two miles). However, he then appears to have become disorientated, possibly confusing the great six-mile line of reservoirs running down the Lea Valley from Waltham to Walthamstow with the line of the River Thames. For in his report he stated that he was flying a little to the north of the Thames and began his bombing run between Blackfriars and London Bridges. Perhaps the roads running between the reservoirs added to his confusion, appearing like the Thames bridges from altitude in the dark. The anti-aircraft gun at Edmonton opened fire with no result, then his first bomb, an incendiary, fell at 22.32 as he flew over Lloyd Park in Walthamstow.

Flying south over Hoe Street he dropped two incendiaries south of Hoe Street Station, followed by a string at the junction with the Lea Bridge Road. Here bombs destroyed four flats on Bakers Avenue, and damaged 20 tenements at Bakers Almshouses; three incendiary bombs that landed on the Leyton Tram Depot at about 22.37 caused serious fires. An explosive bomb also landed in the road between the almshouses and the depot, ripping up

The 17/18 August 1915 raid on London: *L.10*
(Oblt-z-S Friedrich Wenke)

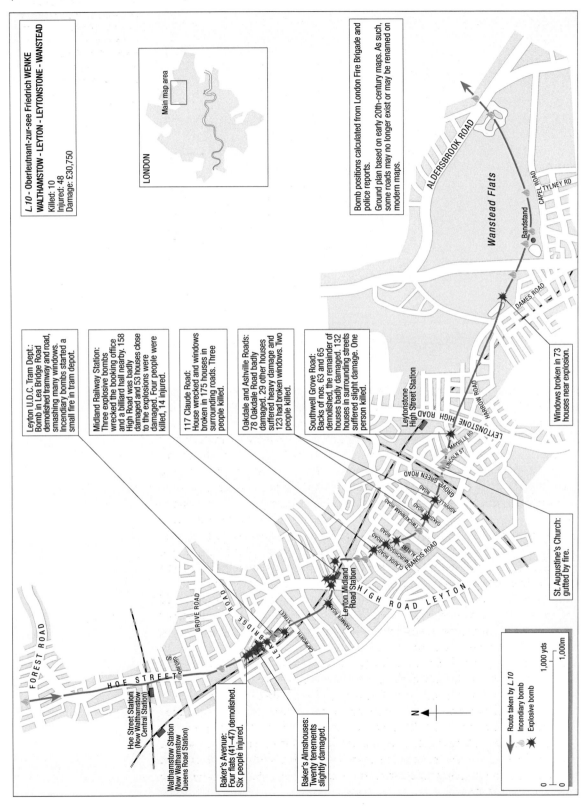

L.10 - Oberleutnant-zur-see Friedrich WENKE
WALTHAMSTOW - LEYTON - LEYTONSTONE - WANSTEAD
Killed: 10
Injured: 48
Damage: £30,750

LONDON

Main map area

Bomb positions calculated from London Fire Brigade and police reports.
Ground plan based on early 20th-century maps. As such, some roads may no longer exist or may be renamed on modern maps.

Wanstead Flats

Bandstand

ALDERSBROOK ROAD

CAPEL ROAD
TYLNEY RD

DAMES ROAD

Windows broken in 73 houses near explosion.

St. Augustine's Church: gutted by fire.

Leytonstone High Street Station

LEYTONSTONE HIGH ROAD

MAYVILLE RD
LINCOLN ST
GROVE GREEN ROAD
ASHVILLE ROAD
OAKDALE ROAD
TWICKENHAM ROAD
MARCHBOSON ROAD
ALBERT ROAD
FRANCIS ROAD
CLAUDE ROAD

HIGH ROAD LEYTON

Leyton Midland Road Station

TANNER ROAD
CAPWORTH STREET
LEA BRIDGE ROAD

HOE STREET

GROVE ROAD

ORFORD RD

FOREST ROAD

Hoe Street Station
(Now Walthamstow Central Station)

Walthamstow Station
(Now Walthamstow Queens Road Station)

Leyton U.D.C. Tram Dept:
Bomb in Lea Bridge Road demolished tramway and road, smashing many windows. Incendiary bombs started a small fire in tram depot.

Midland Railway Station:
Three explosive bombs wrecked the booking office and a billiard hall nearby. 158 High Road was badly damaged and 53 houses close to the explosions were damaged. Four people were killed, 14 injured.

117 Claude Road:
House wrecked and windows broken in 175 houses in surrounding roads. Three people killed.

Oakdale and Ashville Roads:
78 Oakdale Road badly damaged. 29 other houses suffered heavy damage and 123 had broken windows. Two people killed.

Southwell Grove Road:
Backs of nos. 63 and 65 demolished, the remainder of houses badly damaged. 132 houses in surrounding streets suffered slight damage. One person killed.

Baker's Avenue:
Four flats (41–47) demolished. Six people injured.

Baker's Almshouses:
Twenty tenements slightly damaged.

N

Route taken by *L.10*
Incendiary bomb
Explosive bomb

0   1,000 yds
0   1,000m

Lea Bridge Road, Leyton. Behind the railings on the left is Bakers Almhouse. The building on the right is the Leyton Tram Depot. An explosive bomb fell in the road here, demolishing the tramlines, damaging the wall and gate pillars of the almshouses and smashing windows in the tram depot. (C. Ablett)

tramlines and causing damage to the depot. Another explosive bomb landed on the Midland Road Station at Leyton causing significant local damage, and others fell close by as *L.10* continued on a south-east line across the streets of Leyton. Two explosive bombs that dropped in Oakdale Road and Ashville Road killed two people and injured 20, as well as badly damaging 30 houses and smashing the windows of another 123 properties. Wenke then steered over Leytonstone, where three incendiaries in Lincoln Street gutted St Augustine's Church, just a few yards from where Linnarz's final bombs had fallen during the first London raid. Wenke's final bombs landed at about 22.43 on the open space of Wanstead Flats. As *L.10* steered away in the direction of Brentwood those left in her wake evaluated the damage. Seven men, two women and a child were dead, with another 48 people sustaining injuries. The London Fire Brigade estimated material damage to property at £30,750.

Approaching Chelmsford, Wenke released two final bombs, but one failed to explode. The two aircraft that took off from Chelmsford after *L.10* passed on the way to London were still in the air when she returned. These aircraft, Caudron G.3s, were tricky to handle at the best of times and not ideal for night flying. Flight Sub-Lt H.H. Square, flew in pursuit of *L.10*, but was unable to claw his way up high enough and abandoned the chase. Both Square and the pilot of the other Caudron, Flight Sub-Lt C.D. Morrison, suffered bad accidents on landing; both aircraft were destroyed. *L.10* escaped that night, but, as with *LZ.38*, success was short lived. Returning from a North Sea patrol 16 days later, commanded by Kptlt Hirsch, she flew into a tremendous thunderstorm. It seems that lightning ignited leaking hydrogen, causing *L.10* to explode and crash into an area of tidal flats off Cuxhaven; the entire crew perished.

THE THIRD RAID – SOUTH-EAST LONDON TARGETED

Avoiding the period of the full moon, raids on Britain commenced again on the night of 7/8 September. This time the army returned to the fray, with three airships heading for London. A heavy ground mist blanketed the coastal airfields, thwarting any attempts to oppose the raid.

LZ.77, commanded by Hptmn Alfred Horn, came in over the Essex coast at about 22.55 just south of Clacton, but quickly became lost. Having flown erratically over Essex and Suffolk for a few hours Horn eventually unloaded six bombs over villages around Framlingham and departed over Lowestoft at about 02.25.

The other two airships were more successful, though there is evidently much confusion in the reports of the routes they took over London, mainly because they both passed through the same area. It seems likely that Hptmn Richard von Wobeser steered the recently rebuilt *SL.2* in over the coast at Foulness at about 22.35, and took a westerly course over Billericay and Chigwell before turning south over Tottenham and heading for the Thames. Flying over the Millwall Docks at about 23.35, von Wobeser dropped 11 bombs, all of which landed on the western side of the Isle of Dogs, along the line of West Ferry Road. One explosive bomb landing in Gaverick Street demolished three houses and injured seven people. Only one bomb caused slight damage to the dock itself and an incendiary landed on a sailing barge moored off the dock entrance, seriously injuring the two men on board. *SL.2* then crossed the Thames, turned eastwards, and dropped an incendiary on the Foreign Cattle Market, Deptford, which the Army Service Corps used as a depot, destroying some boxes of tea and bags of salt. However, a short distance further on a bomb dropped on the home of 56-year-old William Beechey, at 34 Hughes Fields, killing him, his wife Elizabeth and three of their children aged between 11 and three. Continuing eastwards, von Wobeser steered *SL.2* over Greenwich, where eight incendiaries fell, four of them harmlessly in Greenwich Park. He continued over Charlton where he dropped more incendiaries, and finally to Woolwich where a last explosive bomb landed close to the Dockyard Station. The Woolwich anti-aircraft guns only received notice of the approach of *SL.2* at 23.50 and opened fire two minutes later, loosing off four rounds, but had no time to switch on the searchlight. The gunners estimated her to be flying at about 8,000ft and travelling at between 50 and 60 mph. By 23.54 *SL.2* was out of range, crossing back over the Thames and passing close to the Royal Albert Dock. She headed out on a north-east course, passing over the coast at Harwich at about 02.15 on the morning of 8 September.

Shortly before midnight, as von Wobeser's raid ended, Hptmn Friedrich George, commanding *LZ.74*, approached the northern outskirts of London. Having made landfall over Clacton at about 22.40, George took a westerly course, flying over Mersea Island and Chipping Ongar to Broxbourne. There he turned south and, on approaching London, he released 39 bombs to lighten his ship. George believed he was over Leyton, but his bombs fell on Cheshunt, some 15 miles north of central London, causing significant damage among the horticultural nurseries and large houses that proliferated in the area. The anti-aircraft gun at Waltham Abbey opened fire at 23.55; its crew estimated *LZ.74* to be flying at a height of 9,000ft and travelling at about 40 mph, but the searchlight was unable to get a fix on the target. *LZ.74* continued south and passed out of range of the gun at 23.59. Later accounts suggest George dropped all but one of his bombs on Cheshunt, but official reports indicate that he must have retained almost half his load.

Following a course due south, Hptmn George brought *LZ.74* directly over the City of London. Shortly after midnight he dropped one sighting incendiary in the Fenchurch Street area, causing a small fire in a bonded warehouse. Then, passing directly over the Tower of London, the Zeppelin followed a course towards the south-east, dropping two explosive bombs on Keetons Road, Bermondsey, within half a mile of the Surrey Commercial Docks and, in Ilderton Road, Rotherhithe, another fell on a house let out in tenements, killing six and injuring five people. *LZ.74* then turned towards New Cross, dropping another nine bombs and causing more death and destruction, before departing London on a south-easterly course, reaching the Bromley/Chislehurst area at about 00.35. There, *LZ.74* turned north-east and passed close to the Purfleet anti-aircraft guns, which opened fire at 00.53. The searchlight only caught her momentarily, her speed estimated at 40 mph and height at 10,000ft. The gun ceased firing two minutes later, and *LZ.74* made her exit over Bradwell-on-Sea at 01.38.

In total 18 people were killed in the raid with another 28 injured. However, official estimates put material damage at only £9,616.

This German propaganda postcard published in 1915 may illustrate *SL.2* attacking the Isle of Dogs on 7 September 1915. Most of the 11 bombs fell along West Ferry Road, while one demolished three houses in Gaverick Street and another hit a sailing barge.

The 7/8 September 1915 raid on London: *SL.2* (Hptmn Richard von Wobeser) and *LZ.74* (Hptmn Friedrich George)

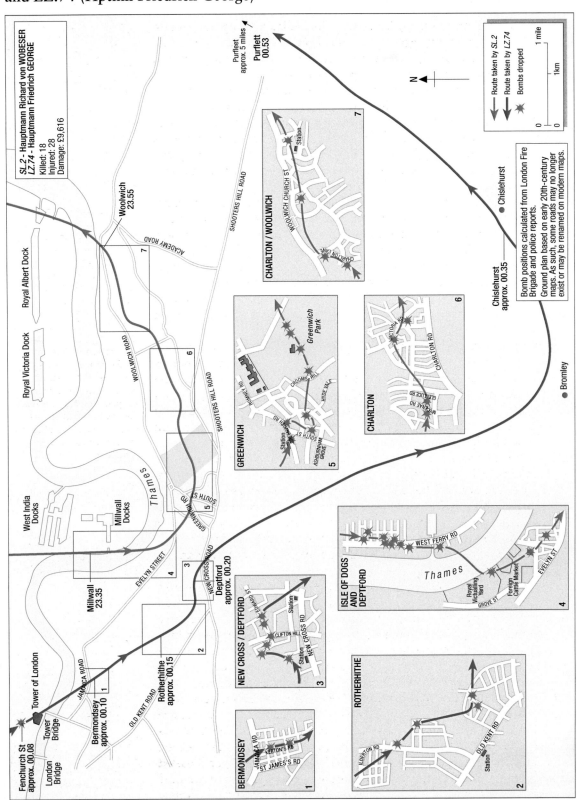

SL.2 - Hauptmann Richard von WOBESER
LZ.74 - Hauptmann Friedrich GEORGE

Killed: 18
Injured: 28
Damage: 29,616

Route taken by *SL.2*
Route taken by *LZ.74*
Bombs dropped

N

1 mile
1km

Bomb positions calculated from London Fire Brigade and police reports.
Ground plan based on early 20th-century maps. As such, some roads may no longer exist or may be renamed on modern maps.

● Chislehurst

● Bromley

Purfleet approx. 5 miles
Purfleet 00.53

Royal Albert Dock
Royal Victoria Dock

Woolwich 23.55

SHOOTERS HILL ROAD
ACADEMY ROAD

CHARLTON / WOOLWICH
Station
WOOLWICH CHURCH ST
CHARLTON LANE
7

WOOLWICH ROAD

GREENWICH
Greenwich Park
ROMNEY RD
CROOMS HILL
HYDE VALE
Station
SOUTH ST
ASHBURNHAM GROVE
5

CHARLTON
VICTORIA RD
CHARLTON RD
MYCENAE RD
GLENLUCE RD
6

West India Docks
Millwall Docks
Thames

Millwall 23.35

EVELYN STREET
GREENWICH RD
SOUTH ST
5
4
3
NEW CROSS ROAD
Deptford approx. 00.20

OLD KENT ROAD

ISLE OF DOGS AND DEPTFORD
WEST FERRY RD
Thames
Royal Victualling Yard
GROVE ST
Foreign Cattle Market
EVELYN ST
4

NEW CROSS / DEPTFORD
EDWARD ST
Station
CLIFTON HILL
Station
NEW CROSS RD
3

JAMAICA ROAD
Bermondsey approx. 00.10
1
2
Rotherhithe approx. 00.15

ROTHERHITHE
ILDERTON RD
Station
OLD KENT RD
2

BERMONDSEY
JAMAICA RD
KEETON'S RD
ST JAMES'S RD
1

Fenchurch St approx. 00.08
Tower of London
Tower Bridge
London Bridge

THE FOURTH RAID –
CENTRAL LONDON BLASTED

The success of the Army Airship Service raid immediately stung Strasser into action. The following night he launched *L.11*, *L.13* and *L.14* against London, while the older *L.9* headed north and bombed the chemical plant and ironworks at Skinningrove, between Redcar and Whitby.

Weather conditions were favourable for once, and there were high hopes of success as the London-bound airships set out. However, only an hour into the flight *L.11* developed engine trouble and returned to base at Nordholz. Kptlt Böcker in *L.14* had reached Norfolk when he too encountered problems with his engines. Realizing he could not reach London, he eventually off-loaded his bombs around East Dereham, 14 miles west of Norwich, then set course for home.

This left the spotlight on Kptlt Heinrich Mathy, the 32-year-old commander of *L.13* – and he did not disappoint Strasser. On his three previous flights Mathy had returned early with engine problems, but this time there would be no recurrence. *L.13* made landfall over King's Lynn at about 20.45. He followed the line of the River Ouse and Bedford Level Canal to Cambridge, from where the glow on the southern horizon illuminated the route to London. From Cambridge, Mathy appears to have followed the road running through Buntingford to Ware in Hertfordshire, before he circled to the north-west of London and set his course for the city.

Coming in over the suburb of Golders Green, Mathy dropped two explosive and 10 incendiary bombs at about 22.40, damaging three houses as he checked his bombsight. Following the Finchley Road for a while, *L.13* then veered off over Primrose Hill and Regent's Park. By-passing Euston Station at a height of about 8,500ft, he slowed his speed to 37mph and dropped his first bomb on central London, an incendiary, which fell on Woburn Square in Bloomsbury at about 22.45. Continuing over Russell Square, he dropped more incendiaries before releasing his first explosive bomb; it landed in the central gardens of Queen's Square, just missing the surrounding hospital buildings, but shattering hundreds of windows. Approaching Holborn, *L.13* released a number of bombs close to Theobalds Road. One damaged the offices of the National Penny Bank, killing a person standing outside; another, dropping outside the Dolphin Public House on the corner of Lamb's Conduit Passage, killed a man standing at the entrance and blew out the front of the pub.

Having bombed Gray's Inn, Mathy then steered a little to the north over Gray's Inn Road, dropping one explosive and two incendiary bombs on Portpool Lane, severely damaging a number of tenements, killing three children and injuring about 25 other people. Twisting to the south-east over Clerkenwell Road, the Zeppelin meted out more damage in Leather Lane and Hatton Garden, and badly damaged buildings in Farringdon Road between Cross Street and Charles Street (now Greville Street). From there *L.13* passed over Smithfield Market and entered the City of London, the financial heart of Britain. Amongst his bombload Mathy carried onboard a single massive 660 lb bomb, the first unleashed on Britain. He called it his 'Love Gift' and dropped it in the middle of his bombing run; it fell on Bartholomew Close, just a short distance from St Bartholomew's Hospital (St Bart's) and blasted a hole in the ground eight feet deep. All around was destruction. Fire gutted a printing works while the concussion of the blast shattered shopfronts,

Kapitänleutnant Heinrich Mathy. Mathy transferred to the Airship Division in January 1915 and became the most successful of all the airship commanders. He took part in 15 raids against England, four of these on London.

BELOW
Queen's Square, Bloomsbury. The small plaque inset in the paving marks the spot where Mathy dropped his first explosive bomb on 8 September 1915. Although hundreds of windows were shattered, none of the hospitals that surround the square suffered serious damage.

scattering battered remnants of stock across the road. Two men emerging from a public house started to run for cover as they saw *L.13* overhead but they 'were blown to pieces' by the blast. The clock hanging in the close offered silent witness to the destruction – it stopped at 22.59. From the control gondola of *L.13* Mathy watched the bomb fall and observed: 'The explosive effect…must be very great, since a whole cluster of lights vanished in its crater.'

Now, having passed just to the north of St Paul's Cathedral, at least 10 more incendiary bombs rained down on the narrow streets surrounding the Guildhall: Wood Street, Addle Street, Basinghall Street and Aldermanbury. However, despite fierce fires breaking out, which gutted at least two warehouses, the historic Guildhall escaped harm. Most of London's anti-aircraft guns had been firing away at *L.13* from about 22.50 with no effect, and an urgent message issued from central control at 22.53 exasperatedly stated: 'All firing too low. All shells bursting underneath. All bursting short.' An official memorandum later stated: 'Ideas both as to the height and size of the airship appear to have been somewhat wild.' However, the guns, and 20 searchlights that Mathy counted, may have proved distracting because he passed within 300 yards of the Bank of England without taking any action. An American reporter, William Shepherd, who witnessed the scene wrote:

> Among the autumn stars floats a long, gaunt Zeppelin. It is dull yellow – the colour of the harvest moon. The long fingers of searchlights, reaching up from the roofs of the city are touching all sides of the death messenger with their white tips. Great booming sounds shake the city. They are Zeppelin bombs – falling – killing – burning. Lesser noises – of shooting – are nearer at hand, the noise of aerial guns sending shrapnel into the sky.

Two buses were hit by bombs dropped from *L.13*. This No. 8 bus was in Norton Folgate north of Liverpool Street Station when a bomb exploded in the road, killing the driver and eight passengers.

Shepherd watched as one shell burst quite close, and someone next to him shouted, 'Good God! It's staggering!', but the airship moved steadily on. Next, *L.13* crossed London Wall, where Alfred Grosch was working at the telephone exchange. He recalls what he saw as he looked out of the window:

> A streak of fire was shooting down straight at me, it seemed, and I stared at it hardly comprehending. The bomb struck the coping of a restaurant a few yards ahead, then fell into London Wall and lay burning in the roadway. I looked up, and at the last moment the searchlight caught the Zepp, full and clear. It was a beautiful but terrifying sight.

Mathy now approached Liverpool Street Station preparing a horrific finale. Just outside Broad Street Station, only 50 yards from the entrance to Liverpool Street Station, an explosive bomb smashed into a No. 35A bus over the driver's head, down through the floor to explode under the conductor's platform at the rear. The driver was wandering in the road in shock, staring at his hand from which a number of fingers were missing, the conductor was dead and the passengers, all thrown to the front of the bus were 'shockingly injured and killed.' Other bombs fell around the station, causing great destruction around Norton Folgate and the southern end of Shoreditch High Street. One bomb landed in the street and blasted a passing No. 8 bus. It killed the driver and eight passengers. Another bomb blew a hole in the roadway over a railway tunnel, severing the water main and damaging the electricity and gas mains. The last anti-aircraft gun in central London ceased firing at 23.00, but as Mathy steered away northwards, the gun on Parliament Hill put a shell uncomfortably close to him as he passed over Edmonton, persuading him to climb to a little over 11,000ft as he turned for home.

Only three BE2cs from RNAS Yarmouth took to the air, but they did not see *L.13* and one pilot, Flight Sub-Lt G.W. Hilliard, died in a landing accident. The damage inflicted was the highest recorded for any single airship raid of the war, London suffering to the extent of £530,787. Amongst the rubble, the bodies of 22 Londoners awaited recovery and 87 more bore injuries that would remind them of this terrible night for the rest of their lives.

The 8/9 September 1915 raid on London: *L.13* (Kptlt Heinrich Mathy)

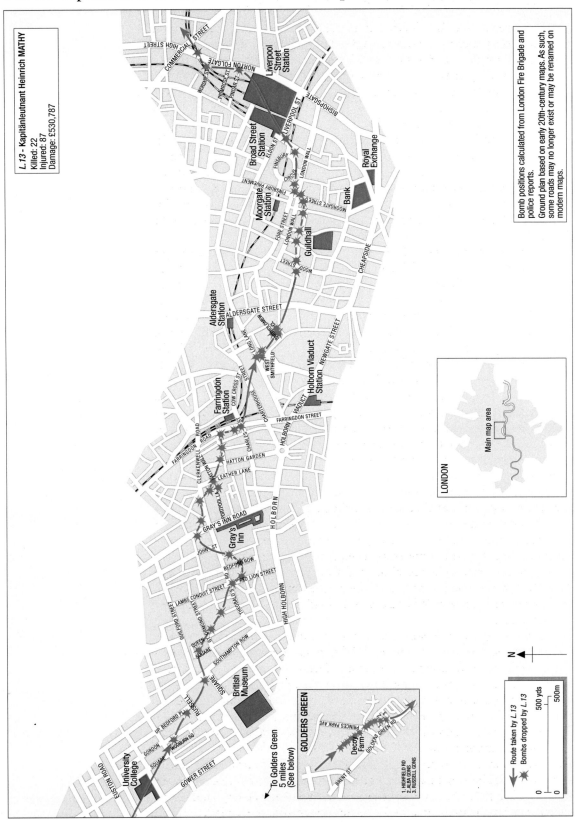

L.13 - Kapitänleutnant Heinrich MATHY
Killed: 22
Injured: 87
Damage: £530,787

Bomb positions calculated from London Fire Brigade and police reports.

Ground plan based on early 20th-century maps. As such, some roads may no longer exist or may be renamed on modern maps.

LONDON

Main map area

GOLDERS GREEN

1. HIGHFIELD RD
2. ALBA GUNS
3. RUSSELL GUNS

Route taken by *L.13*
Bombs dropped by *L.13*

CONCERNS FOR LONDON'S DEFENCE

Concerns over London's vulnerability to aerial attacks increased with each incursion over the capital. Four raids had hit the city, and, during the last, thousands observed *L.13* sailing relatively unmolested over the heart of London. No aeroplanes appeared in opposition, while falling shrapnel from anti-aircraft shells fired at the airship caused more damage on the ground than in the air. Politicians demanded answers, the newspapers posed questions, dubbing the night 'Murder by Zeppelin', and the public felt alone and unprotected in the face of the previously unimagined horrors of aerial bombardment. However, although the Germans predicted that the bombing would cause panic on the streets of the city, they were wrong. It did nevertheless engender a universal anger amongst the population, shocked that Germany could indiscriminately target women and children in this way. From all quarters there arose a demand for a significant counter to the Zeppelin menace.

In response, the Secretary of State for War, Lord Kitchener, ordered Major General David Henderson, Director-General of Military Aeronautics and commander of the RFC, to his office. Kitchener, under great pressure himself, demanded of Henderson, 'What are you going to do about these airship raids?' Even though Henderson pointed out that the defence of London was in the hands of the RNAS, Kitchener promised to hold Henderson personally responsible if the RFC did not oppose the next raid. Accordingly, on 9 September, Henderson ordered BE2cs to both Writtle (near Chelmsford) and Joyce Green and began to overhaul his resources.

Matters were stirring in the corridors of the Admiralty too. In September, in an effort to improve the situation, they appointed the gunnery expert Admiral Sir Percy Scott, recently recalled from retirement, as sole commander of London's artillery defence. Scott wasted no time in attending to his task. A quick inventory told him that his command amounted to 12 guns manned by part-time crews; he ignored the ineffective and outdated 'pom-poms'. He immediately sent to France for a 75mm auto-cannon, a gun far in advance of anything available at that time in Britain. With this weapon, an anti-aircraft gun mounted on an automobile chassis, he formed the nucleus of a mobile anti-aircraft battery. From all available sources, he pressed guns into service and at the same time established fixed gun positions with linked searchlight stations, while recruiting and training the personnel to operate them. Fortunately for London, three more attempted raids on consecutive nights in September all failed and it was a month before a Zeppelin reached London again.

Major-General Henderson meanwhile sent out reconnaissance parties to find suitable sites for new forward airfields positioned astride the north-eastern approaches to London. He secured farmland at Suttons Farm near Hornchurch and at Hainault Farm near Romford, adding them to the RFC roster. In addition, an observer cordon was organized to operate beyond the forward airfields, in telephone communication with the War Office. In a very short time portable canvas hangars arrived at the new airfields, landing grounds were marked out and a group of newly qualified pilots, awaiting overseas postings, reported for duty on London's new front line. Initial plans only required this hastily arranged response to provide cover from 4–12 October 1915, but an extension was authorized. The day after it had originally been due to expire, the Zeppelins returned to the capital.

THE FIFTH RAID – 'THEATRELAND' AND THE ARTILLERY RESPONSE

It had been Strasser's intention to commence raids on Liverpool in October, but the weather forecast for the night of 13/14 October precluded that. Instead, he launched five Zeppelins against London. Alongside *L.11*, *L.13* and *L.14*, Strasser now had two new airships, *L.15* and *L.16*, both fitted with four new 240hp engines, an improvement on the 210hp versions carried by the others. The airship fleet planned to rendezvous over the North Sea prior to launching the attack, but with no sign of Oblt-z-S von Buttlar's *L.11*, Heinrich Mathy, leading the raid from *L.13*, ordered the other ships to move off. They reached the coast of north-east Norfolk near Bacton between 18.20 and 18.45; then at North Walsham, about five miles inland, the fleet encountered mobile machine-gun fire, the new first line of defence. As the four airships continued towards London, the leading trio gradually drew away from Oblt-z-S Werner Peterson in *L.16* and lost contact.

The Admiralty received early advice of the impending raid via reports from the North Sea lightships and increased radio traffic. At 17.30 the six RFC airfields around London received a warning order of Zeppelin activity. This was followed at 18.55 by an order for Northolt, Joyce Green, Suttons Farm and Hainault Farm to have an aircraft on stand-by; an hour later each airfield received instructions to get an aircraft into the air if weather permitted. Thick ground fog prevented any take-off from Northolt or Suttons

Farm, but 2nd-Lt F.H. Jenkins ascended from Hainault Farm at 20.00 in a BE2c, followed 20 minutes later by Lt R.S. Tipton from Joyce Green. As these two aircraft laboured up into the sky – the BE2c taking some 50 minutes to climb to 10,000ft – the Zeppelins continued on their way.

It appears that *L.13* and *L.15* kept more or less together, flying over Thetford and Saffron Walden before diverging near Bishop's Stortford. Kptlt Böcker in *L.14* had already separated from this pair, heading towards the Thames estuary where he intended to pass to the east of London before swinging around and approaching from the south. Mathy planned to circle around the west of the capital and come in from the south-west, while Kptlt Joachim Breithaupt in *L.15*, in his first raid on London, followed the shortest route in from the north.

At about 20.45, Breithaupt approached Broxbourne, Hertfordshire. A 13-pdr anti-aircraft gun opened fire on the looming airship, to which she replied with extraordinary accuracy, dropping three bombs and knocking

Kapitänleutnant Joachim Breithaupt. Breithaupt took command of *L.15* on 12 September 1915, having commanded *L.6* for the previous four months. The 'Theatreland' raid of 13 October 1915 was the first time he had flown over Britain.

LEFT
The scene of devastation at the junction of Wellington and Exeter streets in Covent Garden after Breithaupt's raid. The building on the right is the Old Bell public house. The bomb here killed 17 and injured 21.

LEFT BOTTOM
Lincoln's Inn Chapel. The small white circle in the roadway marks the spot where Breithaupt's bomb fell on 13 October. The blast destroyed the 17th-century stained-glass window above the main arch, and the wall still bears shrapnel wounds today.

Damage caused on 13 October by an explosive bomb at Gray's Inn, one of London's four Inns of Court and home to many top barristers' chambers. (Imperial War Museum, HO.5)

over the guncrew, damaging a Royal Engineer lorry and destroying the officer's car. *L.15* passed over Potters Bar, High Barnet, Elstree and then Wembley, before finally turning eastwards. Releasing ballast, she rose to 8,500ft and headed for the centre of London. As he progressed, Breithaupt kept Hyde Park on his port side until he approached the Thames close to the Houses of Parliament. As the anti-aircraft gun in Green Park opened on *L.15* and two searchlights found her, a journalist watching her progress noted that 'she looked a thing of silvery beauty sailing serenely through the night'. The famous landmarks of London were clear even from a mile and half up in the sky and Breithaupt ordered bombing to commence at Charing Cross Station at 21.35. Just at that moment, an army officer on leave from Flanders was driving along the Strand in a taxi when the driver suddenly came to halt, got out and ran off. The officer looked up at the sky and later recalled:

Right overhead was an enormous Zeppelin. It was lighted up by searchlights, and cruised along slowly and majestically, a marvellous sight. I stood gaping in the middle of the Strand, too fascinated to move. Then there was a terrific explosion, followed by another and another.

The first bomb fell in Exeter Street, just off the Strand, in the heart of London's 'Theatreland'. The bomb hit a corner of the Lyceum Theatre, causing limited damage inside but killing one person and injuring two others

The 13/14 October 1915 raid on London: *L.15* (Kptlt Joachim Breithaupt), *L.13* and *L.14*

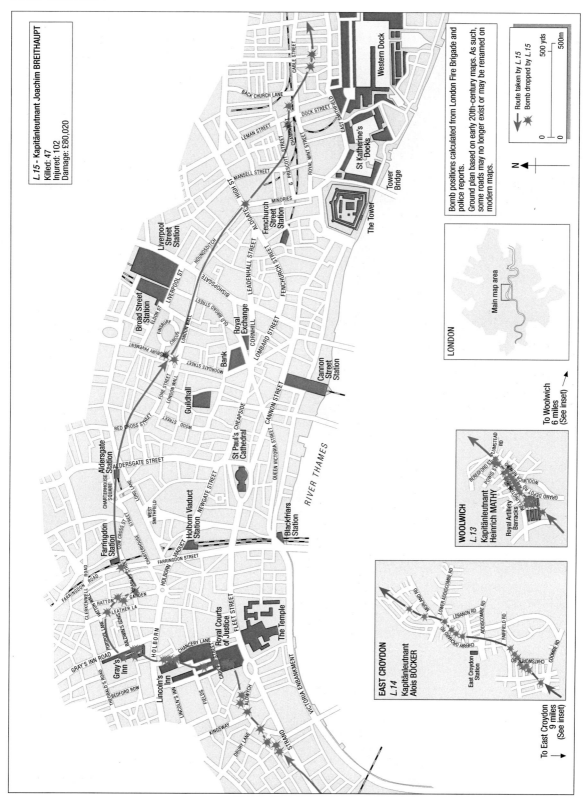

L.15 – Kapitänleutnant Joachim BREITHAUPT
Killed: 47
Injured: 102
Damage: £80,020

Bomb positions calculated from London Fire Brigade and police reports.
Ground plan based on early 20th-century maps. As such, some roads may no longer exist or may be renamed on modern maps.

Route taken by *L.15*
Bomb dropped by *L.15*

500 yds
500m

N

LONDON

Main map area

WOOLWICH
L.13
Kapitänleutnant
Heinrich MATHY

EAST CROYDON
L.14
Kapitänleutnant
Alois BÖCKER

To Woolwich
6 miles
(See inset)

To East Croydon
9 miles
(See inset)

in the street. Another bomb fell seconds later close to the corner of Exeter and Wellington streets. An interval was in progress at the Lyceum and many of the audience were buying refreshments from street traders and at The Old Bell public house. The bomb gouged a large crater in the road and fractured a gas main. As the dust settled, amid the debris, rubble and flames lay 17 bodies while another 21 people sustained terrible injuries. A third bomb fell in Catherine Street near the Strand Theatre. Scenes of devastation and horror confronted the theatregoers as they emerged into the bomb-scarred streets, but high above them Breithaupt continued on his path, disconnected from the trail of destruction below. He later recalled: 'The picture we saw was indescribably beautiful – shrapnel bursting all around (though rather uncomfortably near us), our own bombs bursting, and the flashes from the anti-aircraft batteries below.' Indeed, for the first time a Zeppelin commander was aware of a significant barrage of anti-aircraft fire.

From Catherine Street, *L.15* continued to Aldwych, where two bombs killed three people and injured 15. Incendiary bombs then fell on the Royal Courts of Justice as *L.15* turned onto a northerly course before more explosive bombs fell on Carey Street and Lincoln's Inn, an explosive bomb in Old Square badly damaging the 17th-century stained-glass window of Lincoln's Inn Chapel. Chancery Lane suffered next, then *L.15* crossed over Holborn, dropping more incendiaries and an explosive bomb on Gray's Inn before turning east again and releasing incendiaries over Hatton Garden and one in Farringdon Road, close to where bombs had fallen in the raid of 8/9 September.

Breithaupt now steered *L.15* towards the City of London. Unknown to him, at the very same time Cdr Rawlinson (Sir Percy Scott's deputy) had been involved in a hair-raising dash across London from Wormwood Scrubs to the Honorable Artillery Company grounds near Moorgate with the new French 75mm auto-cannon. He swung the gun into action just as Breithaupt approached. With no time to lose, Rawlinson quickly estimated range and

The corner of Minories and Aldgate High Street. The bomb partly demolished the London and South Western Bank and the hotel above, also severely damaging a restaurant next door. A woman injured in the explosion subsequently died. (Imperial War Museum, LC 1)

height and gave the order to fire. The high-explosive shell burst short of the target, but it was immediately clear to Breithaupt that this was something new. He swiftly released two bombs, which fell in Finsbury Pavement, and started to climb. By the time the gun fired a second shot *L.15* was over Aldgate, where she dropped an explosive bomb that landed on Minories, partly demolishing a hotel, bank and restaurant as well as causing damage to numerous other buildings in Houndsditch and Aldgate High Street. Rawlinson's second round burst above *L.15*, forcing Breithaupt to release water ballast to enable him to climb rapidly. Before turning away to the north, Breithaupt dropped two more explosive bombs, narrowly missing the Royal Mint. The raid had lasted only ten minutes.

In addition to Rawlinson's gun, Woolwich had fired 137 rounds, and guns at Clapton Orient football ground, Nine Elms, West Ham, Finsbury Park, Parliament Hill, Green Park, Tower Bridge, King's Cross, Foreign Office, Blackheath, Honor Oak, Barnes and Waterloo had added their firepower. Percy Scott's new defences had made their presence felt. However, the aerial response was less successful. A combination of ground mist and engine problems contrived to restrict the RFC response, while no RNAS aircraft flew defence sorties that night.

Breithaupt's raid was by far the most successful of the night. Heinrich Mathy in *L.13* had passed to the west of London, but lost his way, dropping 12 bombs around Guildford and Shalford in Surrey, while attempting to locate the Hampton waterworks. Then, flying eastwards, he unexpectedly found himself in close proximity to Böcker near Oxted.

Bomb damage at the rear of 92 Chamber Street, close to the Royal Mint. Four people (Frederick Coster, John Wilshan, Reuben Pizer and Mary Hearn) were injured in the explosion.

The rear of 63 Oval Road, East Croydon. An explosive bomb dropped from Kptlt Böcker's *L.14* wrecked six houses in the street and damaged four others.

A crater caused by a bomb dropped by *L.14* in a back garden in Beech House Road, Croydon. Another bomb seriously damaged the house on the right.

Having crossed the Thames estuary, Böcker in *L.14* also lost his way, flying south until he reached the English Channel at Hythe. Circling over the nearby Otterpool Camp at about 21.05, he released eight bombs, killing 14 soldiers, wounding 12 and also killing 16 army horses. Böcker then turned back inland and, after dropping bombs on Frant and Tunbridge Wells, he encountered Mathy and *L.13* at about 22.40. The two airships exchanged signals then diverged; Böcker headed north-west towards Croydon while Mathy flew north. At 23.19 Böcker dropped 13 explosive bombs near the busy railway junction at East Croydon, but only one caused minor damage to the track; the rest demolished or damaged nearby houses, killing and injuring a number of civilians. From there Böcker turned eastwards intending to head home, but near Bromley, he almost collided with *L.13*. Some accounts claim that the two commanders later exchanged words over the incident.

After this encounter Mathy flew on to attack Woolwich, although he thought he was attacking the Royal Victoria Dock. *L.13* flew in slowly, coming under intense anti-aircraft fire from the Woolwich guns. The first bomb dropped at 23.50 and two or three minutes later it was all over. Although three explosive bombs and over 20 incendiaries hit the artillery barracks and arsenal, they recorded little significant damage. Casualties amounted to four men wounded in the barracks and nine in the arsenal, one of whom later died from his injuries.

The remaining two Zeppelins, *L.16* and *L.11* never got close to London. Peterson in *L.16* lost touch with the others on the journey across East Anglia and at 21.35, as *L.15* was bombing London, he came under anti-aircraft fire from the gun at Kelvedon Hatch, south of Chipping Ongar. Perhaps with memories of the raid of 9/10 August still fresh in his mind, when in command of *L.12* he was forced down into the sea by anti-aircraft fire, Peterson turned away from London and dropped nearly 50 bombs on Hertford, 20 miles north of the city. In his report he incorrectly claimed hits on extensive factories or railway premises in East London. Von Buttlar in *L.11* missed the rendezvous over the North Sea and came in over the coast about an hour after the others. He dropped a few bombs over the countryside of north-eastern Norfolk and returned home.

In all, total casualties for the raid amounted to 71 killed and 128 injured (in London and Croydon the total was 47 killed and 102 injured). Despite the improvement in London's defences, the Naval Airship Division suffered no casualties, although ground fire may have caused some engine damage to *L.15*, contributing to an eventful homeward voyage.

The Zeppelins did not come again in 1915. The arrival of the new moon in November brought the return of darkened skies, but with them came strong gales. Then, in both December 1915 and January 1916, the new moon heralded a period of fog, rain, sleet and snow.

THE 1916 RAIDS

A PERIOD OF CONSOLIDATION

In the lull between the 1915 and 1916 raids, both the German army and navy took delivery of more P-class airships. However, the navy lost the new *L.18* in November, just ten days after commissioning her, in an accident at her home base at Tondern. In December, the first of 10 new Q-class Zeppelins were delivered, five to each service. These new Zeppelins were basically P-class airships with the addition of two extra gas cells, increasing the length from 536ft to 585ft and improving lifting capacity and ceiling. Of more interest to Strasser, though, was the order, placed in July 1915, for the next development in airship design, the R-class, better known in Britain as the Super Zeppelins. These six-engined monsters were 650ft long and increased the lifting capacity and operational ceiling even further.

In Britain, the RFC's temporary defence arrangements for London ended, and by 26 October those pilots recently drafted in to serve on the forward airfields departed to other duties. A number of conferences then took place

L.32, one of the new R-class airships, known by the British as the Super Zeppelins. With six 240 hp engines and a length of 649ft, these vessels were 113ft longer than the P-class and 64ft longer than the interim Q-class.

between the War Office and the Admiralty about the future responsibility for the defence of London. Finally, on 10 February 1916, an agreement stipulated that enemy aircraft approaching Britain were the navy's responsibility. Then, once they crossed the coastline, the responsibility passed to the army – and the RFC. Plans to reinstate October's temporary defence plan for London on a permanent basis received approval and a proposal for the formation of ten home defence squadrons was accepted. The War Office, now responsible for the defence of London, also adopted Sir Percy Scott's plan for two gun rings around London, with a third ring of searchlights beyond them when Lt-Col M. St L. Simon took over the London gun defences.

A weakness in the patrol pattern flown by the RFC during the October raid was recognized and solved. With the second aircraft from each airfield not taking off until the first had landed, a gap appeared in the protective cover. By extending the patrols from 90 minutes to two hours, with the second aircraft beginning its ascent 30 minutes before the first was due to land, this gap closed and ensured unbroken air cover during a raid. Also in February, the RFC grouped all the aircraft assigned to the London defences in No. 19 Reserve Aeroplane Squadron (RAS), with headquarters at Hounslow.

THE RAIDS RECOMMENCE

On the night of 31 January/1 February 1916, before all the defensive changes were in place, the Naval Airship Division launched nine Zeppelins on their biggest raid so far. The primary target this time was Liverpool, but difficult weather conditions and engine failures resulted in the fleet ranging over a wide area of the Midlands and the North, dropping bombs on what seemed appropriate targets. Despite 22 RFC and RNAS aircraft taking to the air, they met with no success in the thick foggy weather, while the rudimentary take-off and landing provisions made the whole process riddled with danger. Only six landed again without incident, and two pilots suffered fatal injuries in crash-landings. The German forces suffered too; Zeppelin L.19, on her first raid over England, came down in the North Sea on the return journey and her crew were lost in controversial circumstances. However, as far as the Naval Airship Division was concerned, Britain lay as open and vulnerable to their attacks as ever.

As the RFC and RNAS prepared for the next Zeppelin onslaught, work continued on the development of weapons to counter the threat. The principal armament remained the 20 lb Hales bomb and a 16 lb incendiary device. In February 1916 a new missile joined this limited arsenal – the Ranken dart – but, again, this weapon required a height advantage before use. More importantly, work was progressing on the development of explosive bullets. Until now the Lewis gun had generally offered little threat to enemy airships, but that would soon change. However, this highly significant leap forward in the war against the Zeppelins was still a few months away.

March 1916 brought another respite for London when the German navy withdrew five of their newest airships in an attempt to solve the recurring problems of engine failure. In the meantime, in appalling weather, three of the older vessels raided the north of England on the night of 5/6 March, causing significant damage, particularly on Hull. Snowstorms and strong winds prevented any aircraft opposition.

A SHIFT IN FORTUNE

At the end of March the Zeppelins came again. This time, on the night of 31 March/1 April 1916, both the army and navy launched attacks. The army airships raiding East Anglia achieved nothing; three Zeppelins set out, but only one, *LZ.90*, came inland as far as Ipswich. She returned home without unloading her bombs.

The navy dispatched seven Zeppelins, with London as their target. Despite four of the most experienced Zeppelin commanders – Mathy, Böcker, Peterson and Breithaupt – taking part, none reached London, although both Böcker in *L.14* and Peterson in *L.16* claimed they had. Böcker, with Strasser on board, dropped his bombs on towns in Essex but claimed Tower Bridge as his target. Peterson falsely claimed hits on Hornsey in north London, but in fact his bombs fell on Bury St Edmonds. Elsewhere, *L.22* – one of the new Q-class Zeppelins – switched targets and attacked Cleethorpes in Lincolnshire, where a bomb falling on a church hall killed 32 soldiers of the Manchester Regiment billeted inside, and injured another 48. The ever-present problem of mechanical failure forced *L.9* and *L.11* to return early, but the journey proved particularly dramatic for the crews of *L.13* and *L.15*.

Mathy, in *L.13* en route for London, attacked an explosives factory near Stowmarket, but a hit from a 6-pdr anti-aircraft gun holed two of *L.13*'s gas cells. He turned for home, losing gas as he went. The crew jettisoned equipment and the remaining bombs to lighten the ship, allowing *L.13* to limp back to base at Hage.

Breithaupt, who had bombed London so successfully the previous October, was not so lucky this time. *L.15* flew in over Dunwich in Suffolk at 19.45, following a course to the Thames via Ipswich and Chelmsford. His route took him directly into the area defended by No. 19 RAS. Notified of the Zeppelin's approach, 2nd-Lt H.S. Powell took off from Suttons Farm at 21.15, quickly followed by 2nd-Lt A. de Bathe Brandon from Hainault Farm and 2nd-Lt C.A. Ridley from Joyce Green. As these pilots urged their BE2c planes up into the night sky, Breithaupt turned towards Woolwich. Six minutes after take-off, Ridley spotted *L.15* caught in a searchlight ahead of him, but several thousand feet higher. He attempted to close and opened fire with his Lewis gun at extreme range, but then the searchlight lost contact, and so did Ridley. When the searchlights picked up Breithaupt again, the anti-aircraft guns on the stretch of the Thames between Purfleet and Plumstead exploded into action. At about 21.45 the Purfleet gun scored a direct hit. 2nd-Lt Brandon had also spotted her and, as she turned away from the guns and lights, he set an interception course. *L.15* started to lose height and the crew quickly established that two gas cells were virtually empty and two others leaking; to lighten the ship over 40 bombs were dropped on open ground near Rainham. At about 21.55 Brandon closed with *L.15* over Ingatestone, about 15 miles north-west of Purfleet, and from a position about

The Ranken dart, a 1 lb iron-pointed metal tube containing explosives, in situ at the Imperial War Museum, Lambeth. Carried in boxes of 24, the pilot could release them all together or in batches. They were fitted with spring-loaded vanes that locked open when the head penetrated the outer envelope of the airship.

300 or 400ft above, he released three Ranken darts as the machine guns on the upper platform of *L.15* opened fire at him. The darts missed the target, so Brandon came around again and prepared an incendiary bomb, but, fumbling in the dark, he took his eyes off the target and almost overshot. Having failed to find the launching tube, he rested the incendiary bomb in his lap and dropped more darts without result. Turning to make a third attack, the inexperienced Brandon – with only 30 hours' flying time behind him – became confused by the speed of action, found himself flying away from *L.15* and lost contact.

Breithaupt was now free of pursuit, but was in a bad way. Jettisoning all excess weight, *L.15* continued to lose height, and as he approached the coast he began to doubt whether he could nurse the ailing ship to Belgium. At 22.25 he sent a last radio message – 'Require immediate assistance between Thames and Ostend – *L.15*' – then threw the radio overboard and flew out over Foulness. Just after 23.00 the stress to *L.15*'s frame proved too much, and at 2,000ft, following 'an ominous crack', her back broke and she crashed into the sea about 15 miles north of Margate. One of the crew, Obersignalmaat Willy Albrecht drowned; the others clambered up onto the top of the outer covering and waited. After five hours floundering uncomfortably at sea, a British destroyer rescued Breithaupt and the surviving 16 members of the crew, taking them to Chatham as prisoners of war. Attempts to tow *L.15* failed and the wreckage finally sank off Westgate, near Margate.

The attack of 31 March/1 April marked the start of a run of five consecutive nights of raiding. Three of these were targeted on London, but because of strong winds only one airship, army Zeppelin *LZ.90* commanded by Oblt Ernst Lehmann, got close. On 2 April he dropped 65 incendiary and 25 explosive bombs as he approached Waltham Abbey, causing only minimal damage to a farm, breaking windows, roof tiles and killing three chickens. Then, just after midnight, as the Waltham Abbey anti-aircraft guns opened up with a heavy bombardment, Lehmann turned for home. Seven aircraft from No. 19 RAS took off to intercept *LZ.90* but only one claimed a sighting.

Strasser realized his raids were not having the effect he had originally anticipated, but he retained absolute belief that his airships would eventually bring Britain to its knees. To ensure he retained the support he needed, Strasser allowed the issue of reports such as that released to the Kaiser after the raid of 31 March/1 April. It falsely claimed success against specific targets in London including an aeroplane hangar in Kensington, a ship near Tower Bridge, fires in West India Docks and explosions at Surrey Docks as well as the destruction of a munitions boat at Tilbury Docks with massive casualties.

REORGANIZATION AND RE-ARMAMENT

In March 1916 the London air defences were placed under the new No. 18 Wing, commanded by Lt-Col Fenton Vesey Holt. Three weeks later, on 15 April, No. 19 RAS became No. 39 (Home Defence) Squadron. Its various detachments, currently spread around the outskirts of London, were concentrated at Suttons Farm and Hainault Farm. The headquarters flight remained for the time being at Hounslow, where all training continued to take place until a new airfield could be located north-east of London. As the squadron quickly began to take shape, it received the welcome news in June that home defence squadrons were finally able to divorce themselves entirely from training responsibilities, which they had until now combined with their defensive duties. With this positive change they became part of No. 16 Wing, which in July was simply designated Home Defence Wing.

While these pilots honed their skills, elsewhere technical developments were finally about to provide them with a weapon to strike fear into the hearts of the Zeppelin crews. Unknown to those men, who flew into battle suspended beneath more than a million cubic feet of highly inflammable hydrogen gas, British aircraft would soon be hunting them armed with machine guns firing deadly explosive bullets.

Initial trials of John Pomeroy's explosive bullet in June 1915 failed to convince the RFC authorities of its practicality. Later, in October, another .303 explosive bullet underwent trials with the RNAS, designed by Flight Lt F.A. Brock (of the famous fireworks family). After further trials in February 1916, the Admiralty placed an order. Pomeroy persevered with his own bullet, and in May the RFC requested an initial batch while ordering 500,000 of the Brock bullet; a similar-sized order for Pomeroy's bullet followed in August 1916. At least one aircraft from No. 39 Squadron used part of the trial batch of Brock bullets in action on 25 April. That same month the RFC also tested a phosphorus incendiary bullet produced by an engineer, J.F. Buckingham. All these bullets needed further enhancement and none stood out as being superior to the others, but they showed great promise. Orders for the Buckingham bullet followed too, and in June 1916 a new tracer bullet, the Sparklet, was added to the arsenal, developed by the makers of the Sparklet soda siphon.

AN AIRFIELD AT NIGHT – ZEPPELIN ALERT! (pp. 52–53)

An RFC pilot **(1)** is shown here preparing for a Zeppelin patrol in early 1916. The devastating Zeppelin raids of September 1915 led to an urgent demand for the RFC to do more to oppose future raids. Accordingly, land was sought for two new airfields on the north-eastern approaches to London. Suitable farmland was acquired in Essex near Hornchurch at Suttons Farm, designated Landing Ground No. II, and Hainault Farm, near Romford, designated Landing Ground III. Suttons Farm comprised 90 acres of corn stubble bounded by low hedges.

Two BE2c aircraft **(2)** were dispatched to Suttons Farm, with one pilot to be on stand-by each night for anti-Zeppelin duty.

Besides carrying bombs fixed in racks under the wings, the BE2c also carried an upward-firing Lewis gun **(3)**. Two canvas hangars **(4)** designated for Suttons Farm were erected on 3 October and a landing ground marked, outlined with flares. Initially these were just old petrol cans with the tops cut off, half filled with petrol and cotton waste then set alight **(5)**. By arranging the lines of flares in a specific order, individual landing grounds could be identified by disorientated pilots from the air. Although originally intended only as a temporary airfield, Suttons Farm became a permanent base, eventually home to No. 39 (Home Defence) Squadron – the most successful Zeppelin fighting squadron of the war.

THE LAST RAIDS OF SPRING

Bad weather thwarted an attempt by naval Zeppelins to attack London on the night of 24/25 April 1916. The following day the army sent five Zeppelins on a course for the city. Despite good weather, only Hptmn Erich Linnarz, the man who had captained *LZ.38* on the first successful bombing of London 11 months earlier, came close to reaching the target. Linnarz now commanded *LZ.97*, one of the new Q-class Zeppelins, and was determined to reach London again. Coming in over West Mersea at about 22.00 on 25 April, he followed the course of the Blackwater river inland. Passing Chelmsford, he headed west until, at about 22.45, he dropped over 40 incendiary bombs on a line from Fyfield to Chipping Ongar in Essex. These caused virtually no damage. Then, 15 minutes later, having steered a south-west course and believing he was over London, Linnarz began to bomb again. His second-in-command, Oblt Lampel, recalled the feelings of the crew at that moment:

2nd Lieutenant William Leefe Robinson. Robinson transferred from the Worcestershire Regiment to the RFC in March 1915. After initially serving as an observer in No. 4 Squadron in France, he qualified as a pilot at Upavon in September 1915.

> [The Commander's] hand is on the buttons and levers. 'Let go!' he cries. The first bomb has fallen on London! We lean over the side. What a cursed long time it takes between release and impact while the bomb travels those thousands of feet! We fear that it has proved a 'dud' – until the explosion reassures us. Already we have frightened them; away goes the second, an incendiary bomb. It blazes up underneath and sets fire to something, thereby giving us a point by which to calculate our drift and ground speed.

But Linnarz's crew had miscalculated, and this second batch of bombs actually dropped over Barkingside, some eight miles north-east of the City. *LZ.97* followed a curving route southwards towards Newbury Park as searchlights flicked to and fro across the sky. Oberleutnant Lampel described them 'reaching after us like gigantic spiders' legs; right, left and all around.' Then the guns opened up. *LZ.97* circled over Seven Kings then headed back towards the east, dropping a single bomb on Chadwell Heath.

However, Linnarz was not yet out of danger. Barkingside lay in the midst of the airfields of the newly organized No. 39 Squadron. With word of the Zeppelin's approach, two aircraft took off from both Suttons Farm and Hainault Farm. Captain A.T. Harris (later Air Marshal Arthur 'Bomber' Harris), commanding B Flight at Suttons Farm, was first up at 22.30 and 15–20 minutes later he saw the searchlights reaching out to the north. At 7,000ft he observed *LZ.97* turning and climbing over Seven Kings. Struggling up to 12,000ft, Harris made for the Zeppelin, which passed over him 2,000ft higher up. In spite of the long range, he opened fire with his Lewis gun, but almost immediately the new Brock explosive ammunition jammed. He turned, got behind Linnarz's ship, cleared his gun and fired again – but once more it jammed. Then, as he worked to clear it a second time, his BE2c slipped off course and the target disappeared into the blackness of the night.

The other pilot from Suttons Farm, 2nd-Lt William Leefe Robinson, took off about 15 minutes after Harris. Then, having climbed to 7,000ft and attracted by the sweeping searchlights, he caught sight of *LZ.97*. Climbing towards her, he opened fire, but estimated the target to be 2,000ft or more above him. Three times he got into position below *LZ.97*, but each time his gun jammed; he fired off only 20 rounds before losing sight of her. Linnarz and *LZ.97* escaped, but it was a sobering experience for Oblt Lampel who later wrote: 'It is difficult to understand how we managed to survive the storm of shell and shrapnel.'

After the departure of *LZ.97*, the skies over London were empty for many weeks. The navy Zeppelins' commitment to the German fleet in connection with the Battle of Jutland (31 May–1 June 1916) and then the advent of short summer nights prevented any more raids on Britain for almost three months.

LONDON'S AERIAL DEFENCE MAKES READY

With this lull in the German offensive, the RFC was able to continue its reorganization. However, in June 1916, with the approach of the Allied offensive on the Somme, the demands for more aircraft on the Western Front led to a reduction in the February home defence proposal from ten to eight squadrons, but even then less than half the aircraft required were available to bring these squadrons up to strength. Further pressure reduced this force again in July to six squadrons, with the promise of additional squadrons later in the year to compensate. No. 39 Squadron was in fact one of the few up to full strength, with 24 aircraft including six of the new BE12. This single-seat version of the BE2c had an improved engine, giving it a better rate of climb and, for the first time on home defence, a Vickers machine gun fitted with interrupter gear. This allowed firing through the propeller arc – a major improvement on the upward-firing, bracket-mounted Lewis used on the BE2c. In August, No. 39 Squadron finally grouped all three flights on the north-eastern approaches to London as the Hounslow flight took up residence at a new airfield at North Weald Bassett.

At the end of June positive feedback on RFC trials of the new explosive bullets paved the way for pilots to discard bombs from their armament. The recommended load for a BE2c pilot was now a Lewis gun firing a mixture of explosive, incendiary and tracer ammunition along with a box of Ranken darts. However, the RNAS steadfastly refused to abandon bombs entirely.

On the ground, although great improvements were apparent in the number of guns and searchlights available, at 271 guns and 258 searchlights these figures remained far short of the national planned levels of 490 each.

RETURN OF THE RAIDERS

The navy airships returned to the offensive on the night of 28/29 July. This raid was remarkable only in the fact that it saw the arrival over England of the first R-class or Super Zeppelin, *L.31*, commanded by Heinrich Mathy. In the pipeline for over a year, the design had suffered a number of production delays, but finally it was ready. At some 650ft long and with a diameter of 78ft, its 19 gas cells contained almost 2 million cubic feet of hydrogen, a vast increase over the 1.2 million of the Q-class and the 1.1 million of the P-class. This increase in gas capacity allowed the Super Zeppelins to climb to 17,400ft. However, at an operational height of 13,000ft the six engines could reach 60mph when loaded with between three and four tons of bombs. While hopes were high for this long-awaited addition to the Zeppelin fleet, their arrival over Britain coincided with the introduction of explosive bullets to home defence squadrons.

This 10-Zeppelin raid caused virtually no damage. Mechanical problems caused four to return early and fog severely restricted the impact of the others.

The 24/25 August 1916 raid on London: *L.31* (Kptlt Heinrich Mathy)

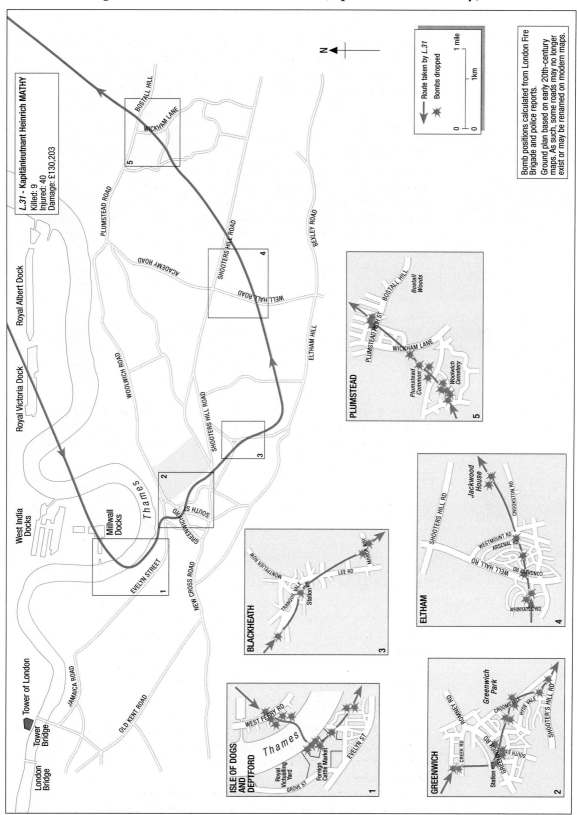

N

Route taken by *L.31*

Bombs dropped

0   1km

0   1 mile

Bomb positions calculated from London Fire Brigade and police reports.

Ground plan based on early 20th-century maps. As such, some roads may no longer exist or may be renamed on modern maps.

L.31 - Kapitänleutnant Heinrich MATHY

Killed: 9
Injured: 40
Damage: £130,203

Tower of London

Tower Bridge

London Bridge

JAMAICA ROAD

OLD KENT ROAD

West India Docks

Millwall Docks

Royal Victoria Dock

Royal Albert Dock

Thames

EVELYN STREET

NEW CROSS ROAD

GREENWICH RD

SOUTH ST

WOOLWICH ROAD

SHOOTERS HILL ROAD

ACADEMY ROAD

PLUMSTEAD ROAD

WELL HALL ROAD

ELTHAM HILL

BEXLEY ROAD

WICKHAM LANE

BOSTALL HILL

1

2

3

4

5

ISLE OF DOGS AND DEPTFORD

WEST FERRY RD

Thames

Royal Victualling Yard

Foreign Cattle Market

GROVE ST

EVELYN ST

1

BLACKHEATH

MONTPELIER ROW

TRANQUIL VALE

Station

LEE RD

MANOR WAY

3

GREENWICH

CREEK RD

ROMNEY RD

Greenwich Park

CROOMS HILL

HYDE VALE

SOUTH ST

GREENWICH RD

Station

SHOOTER'S HILL RD

2

ELTHAM

SHOOTERS HILL RD

Jackwood House

CROOKSTON RD

WESTMOUNT RD

ARSENAL RD

WELL HALL RD

CONGROVE RD

WHINYATES RD

4

PLUMSTEAD

PLUMSTEAD HIGH ST

BOSTALL HILL

Bostall Woods

WICKHAM LANE

Plumstead Common

Woolwich Cemetery

5

Zeppelin *L.31* was the first Super Zeppelin to appear over Britain on 28 July 1916. The photo shows *L.31* flying over the German battleship *Ostfriesland*, one of those that bombarded Scarborough, Hartlepool and Whitby in December 1914.

However, it proved a useful exercise for Mathy and his new ship. Eight naval Zeppelins followed up with a raid two days later. All headed for the east coast, accept Mathy in *L.31* who steered for London, but unpredicted high winds disrupted the attack leaving *L.31* to wander briefly over Kent before returning to Nordholz. The naval airships set out again on the night of 2/3 August. Following a similar pattern, five headed for East Anglia as Mathy in *L.31* made another strike for London. As in the previous raid, Mathy only reached Kent, where vigorous defensive fire from batteries on the south coast forced him away.

Mathy was joined by another of the Super Zeppelins – *L.30*, commanded by Horst von Buttlar, now promoted to Kapitänleutnant – on the night of 8/9 August, when nine naval airships raided the north-east coast, Hull in particular suffering badly. A short lull followed as the cycle of the full moon passed; then, on the night of 24/25 August the navy Zeppelins returned.

THE SIXTH LONDON RAID – THE SUPER ZEPPELINS REACH THE CAPITAL

Thirteen naval Zeppelins set out on the sixth London raid. *L.16* and *L.21* came in over Suffolk and Essex, where they caused minor damage before turning for home. *L.32*, another Super Zeppelin on its first raid over England and with Strasser on board, reached Kent. Greatly delayed by strong winds at altitude, the commander, Werner Peterson, decided it was too late to strike for London, so having flown along the coast from Folkestone to Deal he dumped his bombs at sea and returned. Nine others dropped out with mechanical difficulties or through delays caused by the strong winds. Only one airship made for London: *L.31* commanded by Heinrich Mathy.

Mathy appeared off Margate at 23.30, and for once the bad weather worked in his favour. The night was wet with extensive low cloud, and, although the engines could be heard, *L.31* became visible only momentarily between gaps in the cloud. Mathy followed the line of the Thames and, having passed between North Woolwich and Beckton, he turned south-west over Blackwall. This took him over the Millwall Docks on the Isle of Dogs

The result of *L.31*'s bomb on 210 Well Hall Road, Eltham in the early hours of 25 August 1916. The explosion killed a munitions worker, Frederick Allen, his wife Annie and their 11-year-old daughter Gladys, as well as their lodger Annie Tunnell, whose husband was serving in France. (Imperial War Museum, HO 92)

where he dropped his first bombs on or adjoining West Ferry Road. These destroyed a number of small houses and an engineering works, falling only a few yards from those dropped by *SL.2* on 7 September 1915. Crossing to the south bank of the Thames, bombs fell in Deptford on the Foreign Cattle Market, home to the Army Service Corps' No. 1 Reserve Depot. They also caused severe damage to the London Electric Supply Company and the Deptford Dry Dock. Mathy continued, following the south bank of the Thames back to the east until, over Norway Street in Greenwich, he turned south and dropped bombs on the railway station. The following morning the stationmaster turned up for work proudly displaying 'a wonderful black eye' and a face covered with scores of minute cuts, caused by a shower of stone and shell fragments when the bomb exploded. Besides causing much damage to the station, the bomb also blasted a hole in the wall of the public house opposite and inflicted superficial damage on a cluster of almshouses. Other houses in Greenwich suffered too as *L.31* passed over towards Blackheath; there, an explosive bomb partly demolished a shop and house in the inappropriately named Tranquil Vale. Three other explosive bombs and an incendiary fell on the Horse Reserve Depot of the Army Service Corps, injuring 14 soldiers. From Blackheath *L.31* continued to Eltham, where a bomb blasted a house in Well Hall Road, killing the occupants. Mathy then steered a north-east course, dropping bombs on Plumstead, where one demolished a house at 3 Bostall Hill, killing a family of three.

The raid commenced just after 01.30 on the morning of 25 August and was over about ten minutes later, during which time 36 explosive and eight incendiary bombs rained down. The low cloud made it very difficult for the ground defences to home in on *L.31* and it appears that no searchlights located her until she passed over Eltham. Only after *L.31* had completed its path of destruction across south-east London did the anti-aircraft guns begin to blast the first of 120 rounds skywards. However, one observer reported that all shells were bursting over the target. Second-Lieutenant J.I. MacKay of No. 39 Squadron was the only RFC pilot to catch even a brief glimpse of *L.31* that night, before Mathy headed for home; he was pursued out to sea by two RNAS pilots from Eastchurch and Manston.

Although the raid of 24/25 August had successfully reached London, it failed to penetrate the heart of the city. Instead, the bombs fell largely on poor housing on the south-east outskirts, although the damage was estimated at £130,000 – the greatest single damage caused by the bombs dropping on the workshops, offices and stores of Le Bas & Co, an industrial company based in West Ferry Road. Altogether nine civilians died and about 40 soldiers and civilians were injured. As far as Strasser was concerned, this marked the start of a big effort for the raiding period planned between 20 August and 6 September. However, *L.31* would not be available for service again for another month, as a rough landing necessitated extensive repairs.

Another raid had come and gone. While the increased gunfire offered the public some comfort, what they really wanted to see was a Zeppelin, one of the 'baby-killers', brought down before their own eyes. Wealthy industrialists and newspaper editors offered up monetary rewards for the first Zeppelin brought down over Britain, but that goal remained illusive.

THE TIDE TURNS – THE LOSS OF *SL.11*

Strasser's next big raid, aimed at London on 2/3 September, coincided with one planned by the army. That night, a total of 12 navy airships (11 Zeppelin and a Schütte-Lanz) and four army airships (three Zeppelin and a Schütte-Lanz) set out to bomb the capital. It was the largest single raid of the war, and ended in disaster for the Army Airship Division.

In fact the whole raid turned out badly. The naval Zeppelins encountered rain, hail and snowstorms over the North Sea, widely dispersing their attack. One bombed the East Retford gasworks in Nottinghamshire and another caused most of the night's casualties when bombing Boston in Lincolnshire, while at least six others wandered largely ineffectively over East Anglia. Only

The *Spähkorb* or sub-cloud car of *LZ.90*, in situ at the Imperial War Museum, Lambeth. Favoured by the army airships, these observation cars, manned by a crew member, were lowered by cable to enable observation below cloud formations. This car was jettisoned near Manningtree, Essex during the raid of 2/3 September 1916.

The 2/3 September 1916 raid on London: *SL.11* (Hptmn Wilhelm Schramm)

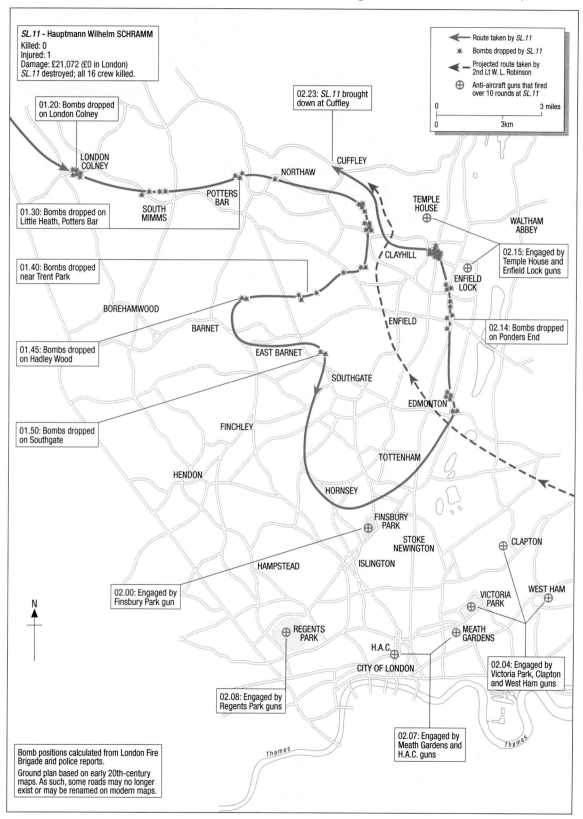

SL.11 - Hauptmann Wilhelm SCHRAMM
Killed: 0
Injured: 1
Damage: £21,072 (£0 in London)
SL.11 destroyed; all 16 crew killed.

Route taken by *SL.11*
Bombs dropped by *SL.11*
Projected route taken by 2nd Lt W. L. Robinson
Anti-aircraft guns that fired over 10 rounds at *SL.11*

0 ———————— 3 miles
0 ———————— 3km

01.20: Bombs dropped on London Colney

02.23: *SL.11* brought down at Cuffley

01.30: Bombs dropped on Little Heath, Potters Bar

02.15: Engaged by Temple House and Enfield Lock guns

01.40: Bombs dropped near Trent Park

02.14: Bombs dropped on Ponders End

01.45: Bombs dropped on Hadley Wood

01.50: Bombs dropped on Southgate

02.00: Engaged by Finsbury Park gun

02.04: Engaged by Victoria Park, Clapton and West Ham guns

02.08: Engaged by Regents Park guns

02.07: Engaged by Meath Gardens and H.A.C. guns

N

CUFFLEY
NORTHAW
LONDON COLNEY
POTTERS BAR
SOUTH MIMMS
CLAYHILL
TEMPLE HOUSE
WALTHAM ABBEY
ENFIELD LOCK
ENFIELD
BOREHAMWOOD
BARNET
EAST BARNET
SOUTHGATE
EDMONTON
FINCHLEY
TOTTENHAM
HENDON
HORNSEY
FINSBURY PARK
STOKE NEWINGTON
CLAPTON
HAMPSTEAD
ISLINGTON
VICTORIA PARK
WEST HAM
REGENTS PARK
MEATH GARDENS
H.A.C.
CITY OF LONDON
Thames
Thames

Bomb positions calculated from London Fire Brigade and police reports.
Ground plan based on early 20th-century maps. As such, some roads may no longer exist or may be renamed on modern maps.

The wooden-framed *SL.11* under construction at Leipzig between April and August 1916. *SL.11*, commanded by Hptmn Wilhelm Schramm, officially entered service on 12 August. The raid of 2/3 September was her first over Britain.

BELOW RIGHT
An unusual photo, showing William Leefe Robinson emerging from the back of an RFC vehicle. On the night of 2/3 September the 21-year-old officer commanded B Flight, 39 (Home Defence) Squadron, based at Suttons Farm, Essex.

three reached Hertfordshire, north of the capital, and these were preparing to strike London when events forced them to change course and make for home. That night the army airships found themselves in centre stage.

Heavy rain squalls over the North Sea forced one of the army Zeppelins, *LZ.97*, to turn back before crossing the coast. Another, *LZ.90*, came inland at Frinton on the Essex coast, penetrating as far as Haverhill in Suffolk, where it dropped six bombs before turning away and flying out north of Yarmouth.

Oberleutnant Ernst Lehmann, commanding *LZ.98*, came inland over New Romney on the Kent coast. Lehmann had almost reached London during the raid of 2/3 April earlier in the year, but the Waltham Abbey guns forced him to turn back on that occasion. This time he approached London across Kent, passing Ashford, Maidstone and Sevenoaks, bearing towards Gravesend. The other army airship to penetrate inland was *SL.11*. Making landfall over Foulness, Essex, at about 22.40, she steered north-west across Essex into Hertfordshire, with the intention of sweeping around London and approaching the capital from the north-west. The newly commissioned *SL.11* was on her first mission; her commander, London-born Hptmn Wilhelm Schramm, had previously led *LZ.93* on two unsuccessful raids against the capital in April.

The British authorities, intercepting a great volume of radio traffic, were aware that a raid was imminent. No. 39 Squadron received orders to commence patrolling at about 23.00. Second-Lieutenant William Leefe Robinson, now commanding B Flight, was first up from Suttons Farm at 23.08 in a BE2c. He began the long climb to 10,000ft to patrol the line from his home base to the airfield at Joyce Green. Within the next five minutes, Lt C.S. Ross took off from North Weald in a BE12, flying the line to Hainault Farm, while 2nd-Lt A. de Bathe Brandon, flying a BE2c from Hainault Farm, covered the line to Suttons Farm. Neither Ross nor Brandon saw any sign of enemy airships and returned to their home airfields, where

A postcard issued at the time supposedly showing *SL.11* over London (possibly suggesting Bruce Castle, Tottenham). However, the image was also re-used to depict *L.31* over London on the night of 1/2 October.

Ross made an emergency landing and crashed. Second-Lieutenant J.I. MacKay took over his patrol from North Weald and 2nd-Lt B.H. Hunt replaced Brandon in the air. At 01.07, 2nd-Lt F. Sowrey ascended from Suttons Farm to take up Robinson's patrol, but Robinson had not yet started to descend. At 01.10, flying at 12,900ft, he noticed searchlights attempting to hold a Zeppelin in their beams to the south-east of Woolwich. The airship was Lehmann's *LZ.98*. Anti-aircraft guns opened on the airship as it dropped bombs and turned away to the east. Robinson estimated he was flying about 800ft above the Zeppelin and, preferring to maintain this advantage, closed only slowly on his target for the next ten minutes. However, his quarry steered into clouds and disappeared from view. Having lost his target Robinson turned away and, sighting the landing flares at Suttons Farm in the distance, headed for home.

At about 01.50, some 15 minutes into his homeward flight, Robinson noticed a red glow over north-east London. Although well overdue back at Suttons Farm, he thought the glow could be the result of bombing and flew on to investigate. He was correct. After his circuitous route, Wilhelm Schramm in *SL.11* set his course for the centre of London and, passing to the south of St Albans, he released a string of bombs between London Colney and South Mimms at about 01.20. Schramm then followed a course to the north of Enfield before swinging around and heading for East Barnet. Then, turning back to the south-east and dropping bombs as he went, he arrived over Southgate at about 01.50. Schramm then steered south, closing on central London, but as he passed over Hornsey a searchlight picked him out and the

THE ATTACK ON *SL.11* (pp. 64–65)

In the early hours of 3 September 1916, a BE2c, piloted by 2nd Lieutenant William Leefe Robinson, attacked German Army airship *SL.11* **(1)**. It became one of the most celebrated aerial duels of the Zeppelin war. Robinson's first two passes were unsuccessful. Because the Lewis gun on the BE2c was fitted to fire upwards, pilots would attempt to make their attack from beneath the target. Observers on the ground noted Robinson's aircraft flitting through the searchlight beams **(2)**, banking 'as it turned almost on its beam ends in wheeling round, in its efforts to secure an advantage over its gigantic foe.' As Robinson manoeuvred into position the crew of *SL.11* opened up with their machine guns.

The top gun platform, merely a shallow recess in the outer envelope, was the most exposed position on any airship **(3)**. It was normal for at least one man to remain here on lookout throughout the flight. This could involve endless hours in freezing temperatures, the only shelter from the buffeting winds provided by a small canvas screen that shielded the guns. Access to the gun platform was via a hatch **(4)** at the top of a ladder that ascended through the structure of the airship. The favoured gun was the air-cooled Parabellum MG.14, firing a 7.92mm bullet **(5)**.

Robinson's third attack destroyed *SL.11*, the first airship to be brought down on British soil.

anti-aircraft gun in Finsbury Park immediately opened fire. The central London guns soon joined in and then, as *SL.11* veered away from the immediate danger and headed towards Tottenham, the east London guns opened up too, adding to the great crescendo of noise over the city. Londoners in their thousands, awoken by the storm of shot and shell the like of which they had never heard before, tumbled from their beds, peering up at the drama being enacted in the night sky. Over Wood Green the searchlights lost Schramm's ship in clouds and, now free of their hold, he resumed bombing as he passed over Edmonton; but, when a searchlight caught him again, the crowds gathering all over London cheered vociferously. Now flying at around 11,000ft, *SL.11* released more bombs over Ponders End and Enfield Highway at about 02.14, before the ever-vigilant Waltham Abbey area searchlights and guns locked on to her.

Robinson already had *SL.11* in his sights. Elsewhere, MacKay and Hunt had also turned their aircraft towards this illuminated target. Following his earlier experience with *LZ.98*, Robinson decided to abandon height advantage and put his nose down to close with the airship as quickly as possible, while *SL.11* attempted to gain height and shrug off the net of light beams that held her tight. At only 27ft in length, Robinson's BE2c was dwarfed by the

Another contemporary postcard depicting *SL.11* held by searchlights and attacked by anti-aircraft guns.

570ft of *SL.11* looming above him, yet some of those watching from below momentarily glimpsed him as he flitted through the searchlight beams. Turning some 800ft below *SL.11*, Robinson flew a path from bow to stern directly under the airship and emptied a drum of mixed explosive Brock and Pomeroy ammunition into her from his upward-firing Lewis gun. To his dismay the burst of fire made no impact other than to alert the airship crew to his proximity. They immediately opened fire, their Parabellum and Maxim machine guns spitting out 'flickering red stabs of light' in the dark. Undeterred, Robinson returned to the attack, this time firing off another ammunition drum all along one side of *SL.11*, but again with no effect. As he prepared to make a third attack a shell from the anti-aircraft gun at Temple House exploded very close to *SL.11* and may have damaged one of the engine gondolas, but then the searchlights lost her again, causing the guns to cease firing as Robinson swung in to the attack.

With the airship now at 12,000ft he took up a position behind her and about 500ft below, before emptying a third drum into one point of the rear underside. For a moment nothing happened, and then Robinson reported: 'I had hardly finished the drum before I saw the part fired at glow. In a few seconds the whole rear part was blazing.' *SL.11* was doomed. Taking urgent evasive action, Robinson avoided the rapidly blazing airship as it started to fall. Lieutenant MacKay saw *SL.11* burst into flames while still a mile from the target, but Lt Hunt had closed to 200 yards and was preparing to commence his own attack when she exploded. In the sudden flare of light Hunt caught a glimpse of another airship less than a mile away but lost her

TOP
The first two postcards in a series of four depicting the last moments of *SL.11* over Cuffley, Hertfordshire. The first image is timed at 02.18 and the second at 02.20.

BOTTOM
The final two postcards in the series. An eyewitness recalled that 'the Zeppelin, now perpendicular, was falling headlong to earth… She seemed to be an immense incandescent mantle at white heat and enveloped in flame, falling, falling, and illuminating the country for miles around.'

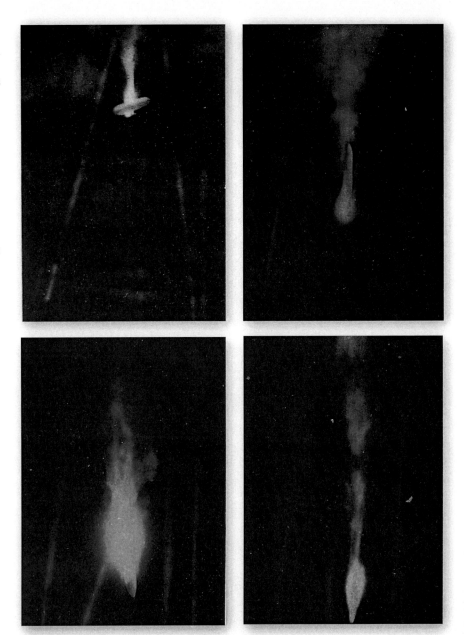

in the glare. This was *L.16*, and her commander, Kptlt E. Sommerfeldt, reported that 'a large number of searchlights…had seized an airship travelling from south to north, which was being fired on from all sides with shrapnel and incendiary ammunition… It caught fire at the stern, burned with an enormous flame and fell.' At least five other scattered naval airships saw the destruction of *SL.11* from a distance and turned for home.

The burning wreckage of *SL.11* came to earth at the village of Cuffley, Hertfordshire. There were no survivors. A vast crowd of Londoners watched the flaming descent of the stricken airship, its flames illuminating the darkness 30 miles away. As it plummeted to earth the crowds erupted, giving vent to 'defiant, hard, merciless cheers.' It was as though the threat of the Zeppelins, under which Londoners had lived since the war began, had disappeared in that blinding flash of burning hydrogen. People danced in the streets, hooters

sounded, bells rang and trains blew their whistles; in the morning thousands upon thousands celebrated 'Zepp Sunday' by joining the great exodus to Cuffley to see the charred remains of the once mighty airship for themselves. Five days later and already an instant celebrity, William Leefe Robinson received the Victoria Cross from King George V in a ceremony at Windsor Castle – and from the various financial rewards he received, he bought himself a new car.

The loss of *SL.11* struck at the failing heart of the Army Airship Service and they never raided Britain again. Disbanded within a year, the army turned its attention to bomber aeroplanes. Strasser, however, was determined to continue the offensive as soon as the moon entered its next dark cycle towards the end of September, still convinced that his airships could strike an effective blow against Britain.

RFC officers carrying the coffin of Wilhelm Schramm at the funeral of the crew of *SL.11*, Potters Bar, 8 September 1916. One woman onlooker, incensed by the military honours given the crew, hurled eggs at the coffin, for which she was later fined five shillings. (C. Ablett)

THE END APPROACHES

Although Strasser remained confident, morale took a further blow with the destruction on 16 September of *L.6* and *L.9*, now serving as training ships, following an explosion in their Fuhlsbüttel shed. In the meantime, the naval crews appeared happy to accept that the wooden construction of *SL.11* may have in some way contributed to her demise, for at this time no one in Germany knew that explosive bullets igniting the hydrogen had been the cause of her destruction.

On the night of 23/24 September, Strasser was ready to launch his airships against Britain once more. In all, 12 were detailed for the raid. Eight of the older airships were detailed to strike against the Midlands and North, while four Super Zeppelins – *L.30*, *L.31*, *L.32* and *L.33* – received orders for London. The only significant action by the northern group was the bombing of Nottingham by *L.17*; the rest made little or no impact.

The Super Zeppelins took off from their bases at Ahlhorn and Nordholz around lunchtime on 23 September. Von Buttlar in *L.30* and Böcker in *L.33* were to approach along the more traditional eastern routes, while Mathy in *L.31* and Peterson in *L.32* came in on the less anticipated southern route over Kent and Surrey.

The first to claim a successful bombing run over London was Von Buttlar in *L.30*. He had previously filed false reports detailing raids on the capital in August and October 1915, and this appears to be another. It seems more likely that *L.30* never crossed the coastline and dropped her bombs at sea. Kapitänleutnant Alois Böcker, having previously commanded *L.5* and *L.14*, was now at the helm of the navy's latest Zeppelin, *L.33*, on her first raid. Böcker crossed the coast at Foulness at about 22.40 and steered a familiar course. Fifty minutes later he passed Billericay and then, turning south over Brentwood, he flew close to Upminster and dropped four sighting incendiary bombs prior to releasing six explosive bombs close to 39 Squadron's Suttons Farm airfield at 23.50. Word of the approaching Zeppelin reached the airfields late and only two pilots got aloft at 23.30; both were still climbing when *L.33* passed over and out of sight.

Kapitänleutnant Alois Böcker. Previously commander of *L.5* and *L.14*, Böcker took command of the new *L.33* on 2 September 1916. The raid on London in the early hours of 24 September was *L.33*'s first and last.

Still undetected, Böcker dropped a parachute flare at 23.55 south of Chadwell Heath as he attempted to determine his position. A searchlight caught *L.33* briefly, but lost contact before any guns could engage. However, the flare does not seem to have aided Böcker in establishing his location, for after continuing to Wanstead he turned away from London. Then, at 00.06, he changed direction again. Now heading south-west, he passed between the guns at Beckton and North Woolwich, before twisting to the north-west and steering towards West Ham. At 00.10 the West Ham gun opened fire as *L.33* began unloading bombs on the unsuspecting streets of East London.

Böcker reported that his first bomb fell close to Tower Bridge, but he was actually approaching Bromley, just over two miles away, where a bomb on St Leonard's Street severely damaged four houses and killed six of the occupants. Steering westwards, he continued his bombing run but suddenly *L.33* shuddered. As the first bombs fell, the guns at Victoria Park, Becton and Wanstead opened up on *L.33*. The volume and accuracy of their fire shook the Zeppelin, even though it was flying close to 13,000ft. It was probably a shell from either Beckton or Wanstead that exploded close to *L.33* at about 00.12, smashing into one of the gas cells behind the forward engine gondola, while other shell splinters slashed their way through another four cells. Böcker immediately released water ballast in an attempt to gain height and turned back to the north-east, dropping bombs as he went. These caused serious damage to a Baptist chapel and a great number of houses in Botolph Road, while a direct hit on the Black Swan public house in Bow Road claimed four lives, including two of the landlord's children. Böcker steered away over the industrial buildings of Stratford Marsh, where his final bombs caused severe damage to a match factory and the depot of an oil company.

The wounded Zeppelin passed over Buckhurst Hill at 00.19 before continuing towards Chelmsford. In spite of the frantic efforts of the crew to repair the shell damage, *L.33* began to lose height. As she approached Kelvedon Hatch, flying at about 9,000ft, the searchlight picked her up and the gun there opened fire, possibly inflicting further damage.

Having been in the air for almost an hour, 2nd-Lt Alfred de Bathe Brandon spotted *L.33* from some distance away as she bombed East London. Brandon, the same pilot who had come close to bringing down *L.15* six months earlier, was unlucky this time too. As he closed with the target, his automatic petrol pump failed, requiring him to pump by hand while loading a drum of ammunition on his Lewis gun and controlling the aeroplane at the same time.

During his attack on *L.15* six months earlier, he ended up with an incendiary bomb resting in his lap. This time, as he raised the gun it jerked out of its mounting and fell, coming to rest across the cockpit. By the time he fitted it back into position, while still pumping fuel, he realized he had flown under and past the Zeppelin. He turned to attack, but, approaching from the bow this time, the two aircraft closed so quickly that Brandon was unable to take aim before the target flashed past.

2nd Lieutenant Alfred de Bathe Brandon. A New Zealander, Brandon qualified as a lawyer in England in 1906. When war broke out he left his father's legal firm in New Zealand, returned to England, learnt to fly and qualified as an RFC pilot in December 1915. (C.Ablett)

The result of *L.33*'s bomb on Botolph Road, Bow. The blast severely damaged a Baptist chapel and 16 shops and houses, also causing slight damage to another four. Two children were injured.

ABOVE LEFT A contemporary postcard showing *L.33*, viewed from outside London, being hit by an anti-aircraft gun shell while over Bromley. The original caption reads: 'A nasty jar for the Baby Killers'.

ABOVE RIGHT A dramatic reconstruction of Brandon's attack on *L.33*.

ABOVE Special Constable Edgar Nicholas. When one of the crew asked him in English if he thought the war was nearly over, he gave the now clichéd reply, 'It's over for you anyway'. (Essex Police Museum)

Undeterred, he turned again and approached from the rear port side, firing a whole drum of mixed Brock, Pomeroy and Sparklet ammunition. Frustratingly, he saw the Brock rounds bursting all along the side of *L.33* but without apparent effect. Loading another drum of ammunition, he turned again, but after firing just nine rounds his Lewis gun jammed. He then attempted to climb above her but lost her in the clouds. His pursuit and attack had lasted 20 minutes.

On board *L.33* the crew were making every effort to keep her aloft. Close to Chelmsford, the crew began throwing any removable objects overboard, including guns and ammunition, but this did not arrest the descent. Böcker hoped at least to get to the coast where he could sink his ship, but already close to the ground a gust of wind forced him down. Shortly after 01.15, *L.33* landed in a field close to the village of Little Wigborough. All 21 of the crew survived the landing; whereupon they set fire to *L.33* before forming up and marching off down a country lane in a half-hearted attempt to reach the coast.

The glow of the fire attracted the attention of Special Constable Edgar Nicholas, who, cycling to the scene, discovered Böcker and his men marching towards him. In a somewhat surreal situation, Böcker asked Nicholas in English how far it was to Colchester. The constable told him, but recognizing a foreign accent decided to cycle along behind them, chatting with one of the crew. Another 'Special' and a police officer on leave appeared as the group approached the village of Peldon and the three men decided to escort the crew to the post office where they found Constable Charles Smith of the Essex Police. Smith formally arrested Böcker and the crew. He then received instructions to escort the prisoners towards Mersea Island and, calling in another eight special constables, this strange group set off and led the crew of *L.33* into captivity.

The 23/24 September 1916 raid on London: *L.31* (Kptlt Heinrich Mathy) and *L.33* (Kptlt Alois Böcker)

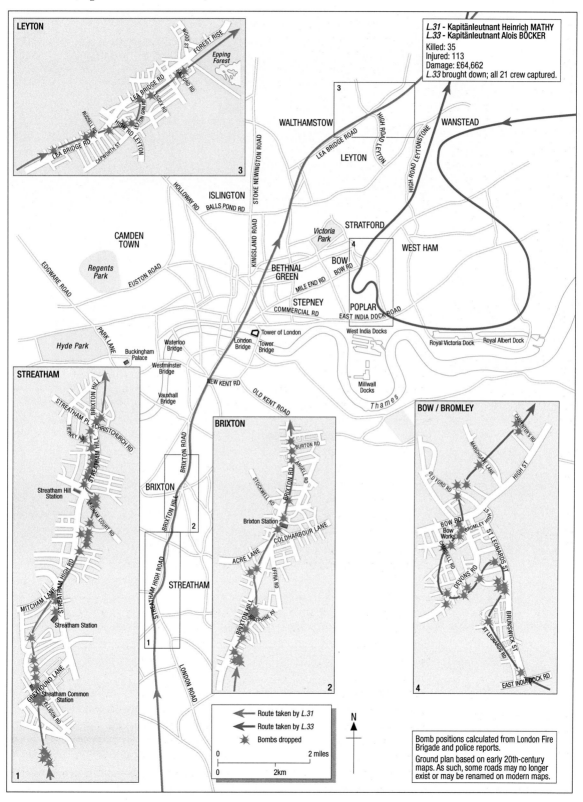

L.31 - Kapitänleutnant Heinrich MATHY
L.33 - Kapitänleutnant Alois BÖCKER
Killed: 35
Injured: 113
Damage: £64,662
L.33 brought down; all 21 crew captured.

← Route taken by *L.31*
← Route taken by *L.33*
✹ Bombs dropped

N

0 ——————— 2 miles
0 ——————— 2km

Bomb positions calculated from London Fire Brigade and police reports.
Ground plan based on early 20th-century maps. As such, some roads may no longer exist or may be renamed on modern maps.

The skeleton of *L.33* by New Hall Cottages, Little Wigborough, Essex. There was so little hydrogen left in the gas cells that the attempt to destroy the ship by fire left the framework almost intact, providing a useful source of information for the British authorities.

L.32 – A SUPER ZEPPELIN DESTROYED

Meanwhile, Mathy in *L.31* and Peterson in *L.32* came in from the south. The experienced Mathy crossed the coastline over Rye at about 23.00 and pursued a direct course for London, passing Tunbridge Wells at 23.35 and Caterham at 00.15. Ten minutes later, over Kenley, he released four high-explosive bombs. All fell in a line, probably intended as sighting bombs to allow the crew to judge their ground speed, but they still caused damage to three houses and injured two people. The Croydon searchlight located *L.31* at about 00.30 but parachute flares, dropped to illuminate the ground below, effectively blinded the crew. At 00.36 lights picked up *L.31* once more and the Croydon anti-aircraft gun opened fire, but another parachute flare caused the searchlight to lose contact again. Mathy flew on for just over five miles before dropping four bombs over open land near Mitcham. Then, over Streatham, he unleashed a murderous salvo of 17 explosive and 24 incendiary bombs. These fell between Streatham Common Station and Tierney Road, to the north of Streatham Hill Station; the blasts killed seven, including the driver, conductor and four passengers of a tram, and wounded another 27. From Streatham, *L.31* followed the line of Brixton Hill, unloading another 16 bombs (eight explosive and eight incendiary) on Brixton, killing seven and injuring 17. Mathy dropped just one more bomb south of the river, which landed in Kennington Park, then ceased as he crossed the Thames near London Bridge. He flew right across the city, the prime target area, and only resumed bombing at 00.46 along the Lea Bridge Road, Leyton, seven and a half miles from Kennington, dropping 10 explosive bombs. Another eight people died here with 31 injured; many houses and shops were damaged. It seems likely that Mathy had miscalculated his position, for in his report he claimed to have bombed Pimlico and Chelsea, then the City and Islington. Flying at 13,000ft (about two and a half miles), he may have mistaken Streatham/Brixton for Pimlico/Chelsea, with this confusion extended as he bombed Leyton. Despite this destruction, local anti-aircraft guns were unable to locate *L.31*; a mist had risen and smoke from fires in East London caused by *L.33*'s bombs contributed to greatly reduced visibility. Mathy steered for home, passing close to Waltham Abbey at 01.00 before turning towards Harlow and following an unhindered course for Norfolk and the North Sea.

The pursuit of *L.33* across Essex held the attention away from *L.31* – and then at about 01.10, as Mathy passed Bishop's Stortford, a vast explosion filled the sky some 20 miles away to the south-east.

Oberleutnant-zur-See Werner Peterson, commanding *L.32*, had approached the Kent coast with Mathy, but encountered engine problems. While *L.31* headed inland, *L.32* remained circling slowly over the coast for about an hour. Finally, at about 23.45, Peterson steered inland, observed from Tunbridge Wells at 00.10. About 20 minutes later *L.32* dropped a single incendiary over Ide Hill near Sevenoaks. However, as Peterson approached Swanley a searchlight illuminated his ship. To distract the light he dropped seven explosive bombs, which only succeeded in smashing a number of windows in the town. However, a light mist south of the Thames helped shroud his movements and no gun engaged him as, flying at about 13,000ft, he moved away and crossed the river east of Purfleet at about 01.00. North of the Thames the mist cleared, and, as *L.32* flew on, the searchlights at Beacon Hill and Belhus Park caught her almost immediately. The guns at Tunnel Farm were first to open fire at 01.03, then, as *L.32* dropped five explosive and six incendiary bombs on the village of Aveley, the guns at Belhus Park, engaged her too. At 01.08, over South Ockendon, Peterson released 10 explosive and 19 incendiary bombs, but the damage they caused was slight. At about the same time another five searchlights locked on and more guns opened fire. Inevitably, all this action in the sky attracted the attention of the pilots of No. 39 Squadron.

Still in the air following his unsuccessful attack on *L.33*, 2nd-Lt Brandon caught sight of *L.32* held in the searchlights and turned towards her. Second-Lieutenant J.I. MacKay had taken off from North Weald later than Brandon, and was about 35 minutes into his patrol when he also saw *L.32*. However, as they both homed in, a blinding light filled the sky as the raider exploded in a roaring inferno.

Second-Lieutenant Frederick Sowrey took off in his BE2c from Suttons Farm at 23.30, with orders to patrol between there and Joyce Green. At about 00.45 and from a height of 13,000ft he observed a Zeppelin south of the

The London Fire Brigade report on the bomb dropped by *L.31* on Estreham Road, by Streatham Common Station, states that three houses were demolished, one partly demolished and one severely damaged. A 74-year-old woman was killed, with nine adults and five children injured. (Imperial War Museum, HO.100)

Oberleutnant-zur-See Werner Peterson. Peterson took command of *L.32* on 7 August 1916, having previously commanded *L.7*, *L.12* and *L.16*. On *L.32*'s first raid on 24/25 August, she got no further than the Kent coast; on 2/3 September Peterson bombed Ware in Hertfordshire.

RIGHT
The bomb that landed on Baytree Road, Brixton, demolished No. 19 and partly demolished those on either side. The house was the home of music hall artist Jack Lorimer. The bomb killed his housekeeper-cum-nanny and the youngest of his three sons. Rescuers pulled the two other sons from the wreckage; one, 8-year-old Maxwell Lorimer, went on to earn fame as the entertainer Max Wall. (Imperial War Museum, HO.98)

Thames. Sowrey turned towards it and gradually closed, as bombs fell on Aveley and South Ockendon. As Sowrey swept in, searchlights still held *L.32*, but the guns were no longer firing.

At 01.10, as Peterson was heading for home, Sowrey emerged out of the darkness, positioned himself below *L.32* and, throttling down his engine to keep pace with the airship, opened fire with his Lewis gun. A whole drum of explosive bullets sprayed along the underside of the vast airship with no effect. As he turned to reposition himself for a second attack the machine guns on *L.32* spat out their bullets in response. Undeterred, Sowrey slid back into a position beneath her and fired off a second drum of ammunition, traversing the belly of the craft, but again his bullets failed to set her alight. Second-Lieutenant Brandon, who had been closing on *L.32*, wrote in his report that he 'could see the Brock bullets bursting. It looked as if the Zepp was being hosed with a stream of fire.' MacKay closed in too. He saw Sowrey empty his first two drums and, although he was at long range, fired a few shots himself. Then he saw Sowrey fire a third drum. This time Sowrey concentrated his fire in one area and a fire took hold inside, possibly caused by a burning petrol tank, for bullet holes riddled one of those recovered from the wreckage. Flames swiftly spread throughout the airship, bursting through the outer envelope in several places. An eye-witness recalled that 'the flames crept along the back of the Zeppelin, which appeared to light up in sections...until it was burning from end to end.' Then, as at Cuffley three weeks earlier, 'the people cheered, sirens started screeching, factory whistles commenced to blow, and in a moment all was pandemonium.' *L.32*

sagged in the middle, forming a V-shape before plummeting to earth in an incandescent mass. Another eyewitness described the demise of *L.32* as it fell:

> Those few moments afforded a wonderful spectacle. Flames were bursting out from the sides and behind, and, as the gasbag continued to fall, there trailed away long tongues of flame, which became more and more fantastic as the falling monster gained impetus.

The burning wreckage finally crashed to earth at Snail's Hall Farm in Great Burstead, just south of Billericay, Essex. Like the Cuffley wreck, thousands made a pilgrimage to see it. The bodies of the crew were collected together in a nearby barn – many horribly burnt. Oberleutnant Peterson, however, had jumped to his death.

Back in Germany there could be no hiding from the fact that this was a serious setback for the Naval Airship Division. With two of his new Super Zeppelins lost, Strasser ordered another raid the following day, but stressed that his commanders should exercise caution if the sky over Britain was clear. Only two, *L.30* and *L.31*, headed for London, but a cloudless sky spelt danger and they unsuccessfully sought other targets. For the next few days bad weather kept the airship crews at home.

L.31 AND THE DEATH OF HEINRICH MATHY

The next test came on 1 October 1916. Eleven naval Zeppelins received orders to attack Britain that night, with targets specified as London and the Midlands. Strong winds and thick cloud over the North Sea prevented four airships from passing inland. Once over Britain the remaining raiders encountered cloud, rain, snow, ice, hail and mist, and this seriously hampered navigation. Only one, Mathy's *L.31*, approached London.

L.31 came in over the Suffolk coast near Lowestoft at about 20.00 and followed a course for London. As he approached Chelmsford at about 21.45, the searchlight at Kelvedon Hatch locked on to Mathy's ship. Turning away to the north-west, he made a wide sweeping detour, passing Harlow,

2nd Lieutenant Frederick Sowrey. Aged 23, Sowrey had received a commission in the Royal Fusiliers and was wounded at the Battle of Loos in 1915. Having recovered, he transferred to the RFC and was eventually posted to No. 39 Squadron on 17 June 1916.

A contemporary postcard originally captioned 'Hot Stuff' showing *L.32* in flames over Essex after the attack by Frederick Sowrey in his BE2c.

LEFT
The wreckage of *L.32* at Snail's Hall Farm, Great Bursted, near Billericay, Essex. A medical officer reported that all but three of the bodies of the crew were 'very much burned… Several had their hands and feet burned off, nearly all had broken limbs.'

ABOVE LEFT
The decision to jump or burn was never far from the mind of any Zeppelin crew as the war progressed. Peterson chose to jump to his death. The original caption suggests the impact of Peterson's body left this impression in the ground.

ABOVE RIGHT
L.31 caught in searchlights over Cheshunt as the guns at Newmans and Temple House open fire.

Stevenage and Hatfield before turning east. At about 23.10, as he closed on Hertford, he silenced his engines and drifted silently with the wind towards Ware, presumably hoping to avoid the attention of London's northern defences. However, about 20 minutes later as he approached Cheshunt with the engines back on, the Enfield Lock searchlight picked up *L.31*, quickly attracting another five beams. At 23.38 the Newmans anti-aircraft gun opened fire, followed a minute later by the Temple House gun.

This sudden outbreak of gunfire attracted the pilots of No. 39 Squadron. Orders to commence patrolling only arrived a little before 22.00 and the first three pilots were still climbing to operational height as *L.31* approached and passed their patrol lines unseen. As the lights caught the beleaguered airship, lieutenants MacKay, Payne and Tempest all turned towards it. Another pilot, P. McGuinness, who had taken off at 23.25 to patrol a line from North Weald to Hendon, also saw *L.31* in the searchlights about 20 minutes later and joined the chase. But it was 2nd-Lt Wulstan Tempest who caught her first.

Tempest estimates he was about 15 miles away when the guns opened fire. As he closed to within five miles of the target, Tempest realized he was at a height well above the Zeppelin and found the anti-aircraft shells bursting uncomfortably close to his BE2c. Then, as he passed through one of the searchlights, someone on board *L.31* saw his approach and Mathy immediately ordered the release of 24 explosive and 26 incendiary bombs in an attempt to gain height. The bombs landed on Cheshunt, seriously damaging four houses and breaking windows and doors in 343 others as well as destroying 40 horticultural glasshouses. Fortunately for the residents of the town, casualties were restricted to one woman slightly cut by flying glass. *L.31* zigzagged away westwards, rapidly gaining height.

As he closed to launch his attack, Tempest's pressure petrol pump failed and he had to hand-pump furiously prior to making his attack before *L.31* could climb out of reach. He recorded, thankfully, that he was now beyond the range of the anti-aircraft guns – the last gun ceased firing at 23.50. Flying

straight at the oncoming airship, Tempest flew under its belly, firing off a short burst of mixed Pomeroy, Buckingham and standard ammunition with no effect. He quickly turned until he was flying underneath in the same direction as *L.31* and gave her another burst, but again there was no result other than to draw machine-gun fire from the crew. He banked and then sat under her tail, from where the machine guns were unable to reach him. Although he had almost begun to despair of bringing her down, he attacked again and, in his words, 'pumped lead into her for all I was worth.'

As this third burst penetrated the outer skin of *L.31*, Tempest recalled: 'I noticed her begin to go red inside like an enormous Chinese lantern and then a flame shot out of the front part of her and I realized she was on fire.'

L.31 shot about 200ft up in the air then began to fall, 'roaring like a furnace', directly towards Tempest who dived as hard as he could to get out of the way of the burning wreck. Tempest returned to Hainault Farm, but, feeling 'sick, giddy and exhausted', wrecked his own aircraft on landing although he only suffered minor injuries to himself. *L.31* crashed to earth at Potters Bar in Hertfordshire, only a few miles from the scene of William Leefe Robinson's victory at Cuffley.

All 19 of the crew of *L.31* perished. Many, including Heinrich Mathy – the most respected and successful of all the Zeppelin commanders – jumped

TO BURN OR TO JUMP – THE DEATH OF HEINRICH MATHY (pp. 80–81)

On the night of 1 October 1916, 2nd Lieutenant Wulstan Tempest, in a BE2c **(1)**, attacked and shot down Zeppelin *L.31* **(2)** commanded by Kptlt Heinrich Mathy, the most revered of all the Zeppelin commanders.

Since the introduction of explosive bullets for use with the Lewis gun, the advantage in aerial combat had swung to the pilots of the RFC and RNAS. With the realization that they were now extremely vulnerable, German aircrew began to dwell on the last great question – if your Zeppelin is on fire and there is no hope of survival, do you jump to your death or burn in the wreckage? When Heinrich Mathy was asked this question he replied, 'I won't know until it happens.'

Elsewhere, one of his crew confessed that the old cheerfulness had disappeared:

'We discuss our heavy losses… Our nerves are on edge, and even the most energetic and determined cannot shake off the gloomy atmosphere… It is only a question of time before we join the rest. Everyone admits that they feel it… If anyone should say that he was not haunted by visions of burning airships, then he would be a braggart.'

When the time came, with the fire spreading rapidly through the gas cells contained within the outer envelope **(3)** of *L.31*, Mathy **(4)** chose to jump to his death.

The tangle of wreckage that was once Heinrich Mathy's *L.31*. The burning ship broke up and fell in two main sections a few hundred feet apart. This section, guarded by a cordon of soldiers, lies impaled on an oak tree in a misty Oakmere Park, Potters Bar.

to their deaths rather than be burnt alive. This had been his 15th raid over England and his death struck right at the heart of the Naval Airship Division. In a letter to Mathy's widow, Peter Strasser described his fallen comrade as a man of 'daring, of tireless energy…and at the same time a cheerful, helpful and true comrade and friend, high in the estimation of his superiors, his equals and his subordinates.'

ZEPPELIN LOSSES MOUNT

Zeppelins did not return to England again until 27 November 1916, when, avoiding London, they selected targets in the industrial Midlands and the North. Yet the result was much the same. *L.34*, commanded by Kptlt Max Dietrich, was shot down in flames by 2nd-Lt I.V. Pyott of No. 36 Squadron, based at Seaton Carew, and crashed into the sea near the mouth of the River Tees. Further south, about 10 miles off the coast from Lowestoft, the joint efforts of two aircraft piloted by Flight Lt Egbert Cadbury and Flight Sub-Lt Edward Pulling, RNAS, shot down *L.21* commanded by Kptlt Kurt Frankenburg. There were no survivors from either wreck.

An already bad end to 1916 got even worse when three more airships were lost on 28 December. First, *SL.12*, although damaged, survived a bad landing at the Ahlhorn base, but strong overnight winds destroyed her. Then, at Tondern an equipment failure caused the ground crew to lose control of *L.24* as she came in to land, whereupon she smashed against the shed and burst into flames, which also engulfed the neighbouring *L.17*.

Although the army had lost faith in the airship's ability to carry the war to Britain, Strasser, driven by his unshakeable belief and now appointed Führer der Luftschiffe, remained positive. He insisted on new airships of improved performance for the navy, demanding a greater ceiling to enable the airships to operate above the range of the now lethal British aircraft. Indeed, while the overall material effect of the airship raids was limited, by the end of 1916 they resulted in the commitment of some 17,000 British servicemen to home defence duty.

Royal Flying Corps Home Defence squadrons, November 1916

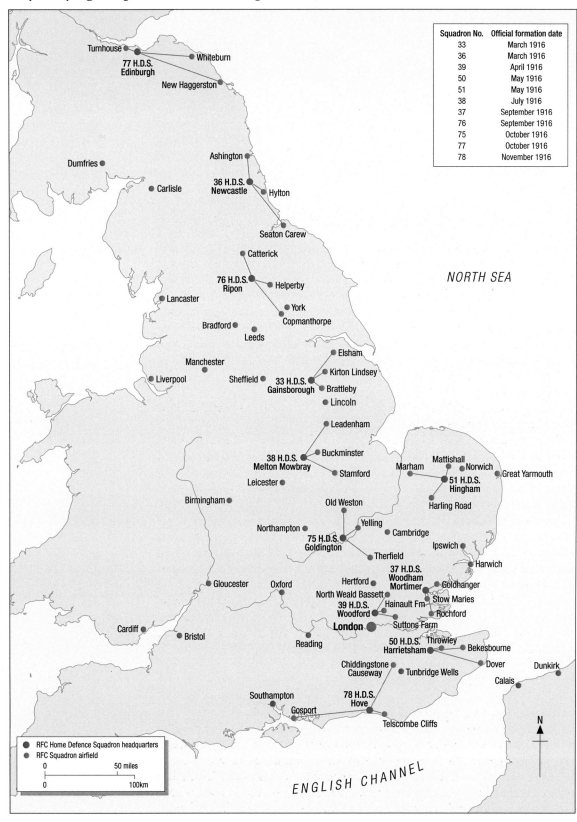

Squadron No.	Official formation date
33	March 1916
36	March 1916
39	April 1916
50	May 1916
51	May 1916
38	July 1916
37	September 1916
76	September 1916
75	October 1916
77	October 1916
78	November 1916

Turnhouse
Whiteburn
**77 H.D.S.
Edinburgh**
New Haggerston

Dumfries
Carlisle
Ashington
**36 H.D.S.
Newcastle** Hylton
Seaton Carew
Catterick
**76 H.D.S.
Ripon** Helperby
Lancaster
York
Copmanthorpe
Bradford
Leeds
Elsham
Manchester
Kirton Lindsey
Liverpool
Sheffield **33 H.D.S.
Gainsborough** Brattleby
Lincoln
Leadenham
Buckminster
**38 H.D.S.
Melton Mowbray** Stamford
Leicester
Birmingham
Mattishall
Marham Norwich
**51 H.D.S.
Hingham** Great Yarmouth
Old Weston
Harling Road
Northampton Yelling
Cambridge
**75 H.D.S.
Goldington** Ipswich
Therfield Harwich
**37 H.D.S.
Woodham
Mortimer** Goldhanger
Gloucester Oxford Hertford
North Weald Bassett
**39 H.D.S.
Woodford** Hainault Fm Stow Maries
Rochford
London Suttons Farm
Cardiff Bristol
Reading
**50 H.D.S.
Harrietsham** Throwley
Bekesbourne
Chiddingstone
Causeway Tunbridge Wells
Dover Dunkirk
Calais
Southampton
**78 H.D.S.
Hove**
Gosport
Telscombe Cliffs

NORTH SEA

N

- ● RFC Home Defence Squadron headquarters
- ● RFC Squadron airfield

0   50 miles
0   100km

ENGLISH CHANNEL

THE 1917 RAIDS

THE ARRIVAL OF THE 'HEIGHT CLIMBERS'

The first of the new S-Class Zeppelins (in the form of *L.42*) entered naval service on 28 February 1917. She had an operational ceiling of 16,500ft and the ability to climb to about 21,000ft (four miles high), way beyond the reach of the anti-aircraft guns and aircraft allocated to home defence. However, to attain these great heights the new models traded against a reduction in power, fitting five engines instead of six. With existing Super Zeppelins also altered to fulfil these new requirements, the British dubbed this new class of airship, the 'Height Climbers'.

The first raid of 1917 took place on the night of 16/17 March, with London as its target. The force, made up of *L.42* and four converted Super Zeppelins, encountered fierce 45mph winds from the north-west that blew them south and none penetrated farther inland than Ashford in Kent.

On the night of 23/24 May, six Height Climbers targeted London again. Adverse winds at high altitude disrupted the raid and no airships reached the city. The closest, *L.42*, turned back over Braintree in Essex, some 40 miles away. All the crews suffered badly from the intense cold and experienced the debilitating effects of altitude sickness encountered at these great heights. Two days after this raid Germany launched its first major aeroplane raid on London, with 21 twin-engine Gotha bombers crossing the Essex coastline in daylight. Only a heavy cloud build-up over the capital prevented them from reaching London, but it marked a dramatic change in the air war over the city.

Having studied the report of the 23/24 May Zeppelin raid, the Kaiser voiced the opinion that 'the day of the airship is past for attacks on London.' However, strong representations from the naval authorities persuaded him to approve their continuation, but only 'when the circumstances seem favourable.' Strasser decided they were favourable on 16/17 June 1917.

L.48 – DEATH THROES

Strong winds and engine problems prevented all but two of the six Zeppelins detailed for the 16/17 June raid from reaching England. These strong winds held *L.42* over Kent, where she bombed Ramsgate before heading for home, but not before one of her bombs struck lucky, hitting a naval ammunition store. The other raider, *L.48*, commanded by Kptlt Franz Eichler, but with Kvtkpt Viktor Schütze (the new commander of the Naval Airship Division since Strasser's appointment as Führer der Luftschiffe) on board,

experienced serious engine problems and her compass froze. Unable to reach London, *L.48* attempted to bomb Harwich naval base then turned for home, dropping to 13,000ft to take advantage of tailwinds to compensate for the lack of engine power. At this height, and in a lightening summer sky, the air defences easily located *L.48*. Three aircraft from Orfordness Experimental Station, as well as a BE12 of No. 37 Squadron, all saw *L.48* heading towards the coast and gave chase. Three of the aircraft scored hits as they swarmed around the lone airship. Minutes later *L.48*, the most recent addition to the navy's airship fleet, commissioned only 26 days earlier, crashed in flames in a field at Holly Tree Farm, Theberton, Suffolk. Miraculously, three members of the crew survived the crash, but Viktor Schütze was not one of them.

L.48, one of the new type dubbed 'Height Climbers' by the British, entered service on 23 May 1917, based at Nordholz. To hinder search-lights, the undersides were painted black. Commanded by Kptlt Franz Eichler, the raid of 16/17 June was her first time over England. (Imperial War Museum, Q.58467)

The Naval Airship Division never directly targeted London again. However, in one of the most disastrous airship raids of the war, the final Zeppelin bombs dropped on the capital on the night of 19/20 October 1917.

THE SILENT RAID

The naval airships had already undertaken raids against northern England on 21/22 August and the Midlands and the North again on 24/25 September 1917 without great success. During this period, the twin-engine Gotha bombers carried out their campaign against London, joined at the end of September by the massive Staaken Giants, designed by the Zeppelin Company. Then, on 19 October, 13 airships set out to attack targets in industrial northern cities such as Sheffield, Manchester and Liverpool; it was the last large-scale airship raid of the war. Two vessels failed to take off, while the other 11 encountered vicious headwinds once they had climbed over 16,000ft. The high winds battered the airships off course and reduced their ground speed to a crawl, making it almost impossible for the commanders to ascertain their positions.

Kapitänleutnant Waldemar Kölle, commanding *L.45*, aimed for Sheffield but found himself moving rapidly southwards and reported that 'precise orientation from the ground was impossible… no fixed points could be discerned.' He dropped a number of bombs that fell on Northampton. Then, just before 23.30, the crew became aware of a large concentration of dim lights extending before them for some distance. Kölle's second-in-command, Lt Schütz, shouted 'London!' and for the first time Kölle realized how far off course *L.45* had travelled. Wasting no time, he immediately released a number of bombs that fell in north-west London, causing damage to the Graham White Aviation Company at Hendon Aerodrome and on cottages nearby. Hendon experienced more damage before *L.45*, continuing on a south-east course, dropped two explosive bombs near Cricklewood Station.

The great height of *L.45*, coupled with a thin veil of cloud, meant Kölle's progress towards the centre of the capital remained unseen and unheard by those on the ground. Therefore no guns opened fire, and the attack became known as the 'silent raid'. One of the crew described their experience over London:

> The Thames we just dimly saw from the outline of the lights; two great railway stations I thought I saw, but the speed of the ship running almost before the gale was such that we could not distinguish much. We were half frozen, too, and the excitement was great. It was all over in a flash. The last bomb was gone and we were once more over the darkness and rushing onwards.

In fact, these randomly dropped bombs proved devastating. The first fell without warning in Piccadilly, close to Piccadilly Circus in the heart of London's West End. The massive 660 lb bomb blasted a hole in the road about 12ft in diameter, fracturing two gas mains and pipes carrying telephone cables. The blast smashed the whole of the front of the fashionable department store Swan & Edgar's, with damage extending into Regent Street, Jermyn Street and Shaftesbury Avenue amongst others. Many people were in the streets, unaware of the impending danger, and were caught in the explosion. Flying shrapnel, debris and glass scythed down 25 people, of whom seven died, including three soldiers on leave. One woman, so disfigured by the blast, was eventually only identified by her clothes and jewellery.

L.45 careered on. The next bomb fell in Camberwell, on the corner of Albany Road and Calmington Road, demolishing three homes as well as a doctor's surgery and a fish and chip shop. Many other buildings were seriously damaged. The blast killed 10, including four children; another 10 children were amongst the 24 people injured.

The final bomb dropped by *L.45* landed in Glenview Road, Hither Green, demolishing three houses and inflicting less serious damage on other houses in the surrounding roads, but it claimed a high cost in human life. The bomb killed another 10 children – seven of these from one family – and five women, while six people needed treatment for their injuries.

The wreckage of *L.48* at Theberton, Suffolk. Two cordons of soldiers keep onlookers at a safe distance as the bodies of the crew are recovered. (National Archives AIR 1/596/16/15/217)

The 19/20 October 1917 raid on London: *L.45* (Kptlt Waldemar Kölle)

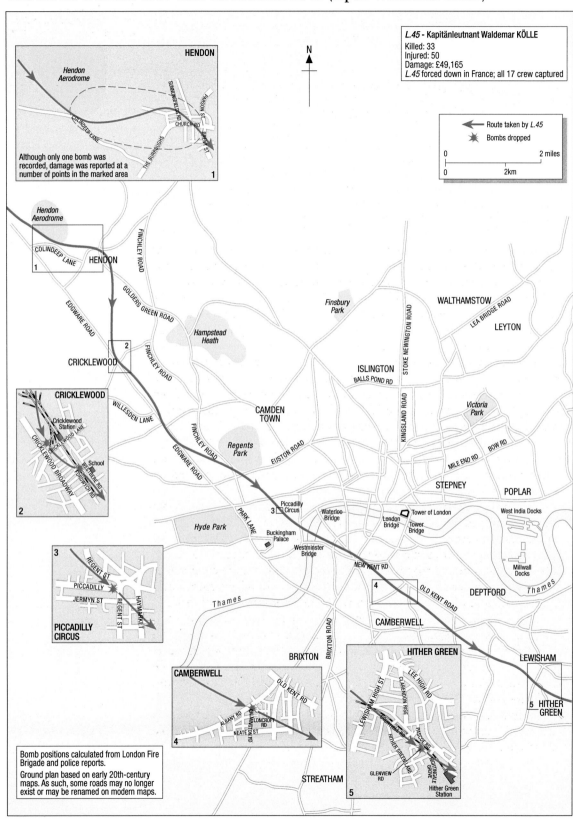

L.45 - Kapitänleutnant Waldemar KÖLLE
Killed: 33
Injured: 50
Damage: £49,165
L.45 forced down in France; all 17 crew captured

Route taken by *L.45*
Bombs dropped

0   2 miles
0   2km

HENDON

Hendon
Aerodrome

SUNNINGFIELDS RD
PARSON ST
CHURCH RD
BRENT ST
THE BURROUGHS
COLINDEEP LANE

Although only one bomb was
recorded, damage was reported at a
number of points in the marked area

1

N

Hendon
Aerodrome

COLINDEEP LANE

HENDON

1

EDGWARE ROAD

FINCHLEY ROAD

GOLDERS GREEN ROAD

CRICKLEWOOD

2

FINCHLEY ROAD

Hampstead
Heath

Finsbury
Park

WALTHAMSTOW
LEA BRIDGE ROAD
LEYTON

CRICKLEWOOD

Cricklewood
Station

CRICKLEWOOD LANE
CRICKLEWOOD BROADWAY
WESTBERE RD
CHURCH RD
School

2

WILLESDEN LANE

EDGWARE ROAD

FINCHLEY ROAD

CAMDEN
TOWN

Regents
Park

EUSTON ROAD

ISLINGTON
BALLS POND RD

STOKE NEWINGTON ROAD
KINGSLAND ROAD

Victoria
Park

MILE END RD
BOW RD

STEPNEY

POPLAR

West India Docks

3
PICCADILLY
CIRCUS

REGENT ST
PICCADILLY
JERMYN ST
REGENT ST
HAYMARKET

Hyde Park

PARK LANE

Piccadilly
3 Circus

Waterloo
Bridge

Buckingham
Palace

Westminster
Bridge

London
Bridge

Tower of London
Tower
Bridge

Millwall
Docks

Thames

DEPTFORD

Thames

NEW KENT RD

4

OLD KENT ROAD

CAMBERWELL

BRIXTON

BRIXTON ROAD

CAMBERWELL

ALBANY RD
NEATE ST
KILMINGTON RD
LONCROFT
RD
OLD KENT RD

4

HITHER GREEN

LEWISHAM HIGH ST
LEE HIGH RD
CLARENDON RISE
COURTHILL RD
HITHER GREEN LANE
PASCOE RD
NIGHTINGALE GROVE
GLENVIEW RD
Hither Green
Station

5

LEWISHAM

5 HITHER
GREEN

STREATHAM

Bomb positions calculated from London Fire
Brigade and police reports.

Ground plan based on early 20th-century
maps. As such, some roads may no longer
exist or may be renamed on modern maps.

88

L.45 was the penultimate R-class Zeppelin delivered to the Naval Airship Division. She entered service on 7 April 1917 under the command of Kptlt Waldemar Kölle. The raid of 19/20 October 1917 was the third time *L.45* had appeared over Britain. (Imperial War Museum, Q.58465)

However, for the crew of *L.45*, their rather precarious position was just about to get worse. Having dropped to 15,000ft to get below the fierce winds at high altitude, Kölle managed to make some headway eastwards. However, near Chatham shortly after midnight, *L.45* encountered 2nd-Lt Thomas Pritchard of No. 39 Squadron, flying his BE2e from North Weald. Only able to get his aircraft up to 13,000ft, Pritchard fired at *L.45* anyway. He missed the target, but Kölle climbed rapidly to escape the pursuer and was caught again in the gales; once more, the wind swept *L.45* southwards. One engine then broke down, and in the intense cold it proved impossible to repair. One member of the crew retired with frostbite while many others suffered from altitude sickness. The winds drove *L.45* across France where she lost another two engines and was fortunate to survive an encounter with French anti-aircraft guns. With fuel almost exhausted and only two engines still working, *L.45* had no chance of getting back to Germany, and so Kölle brought her down in a riverbed near Sisteron in southern France. The crew set fire to their ship and surrendered to a group of French soldiers.

Other ships of the attacking force suffered similar fates. *L.44* came down in flames, destroyed by anti-aircraft guns while attempting to cross the front-line trenches in an effort to get back to Germany. Kapitänleutnant Hans-Karl Gayer brought *L.49* down in a wood in France, where soldiers captured her before the crew could destroy her. Having lost two engines the commander of *L.50*, Kptlt Roderich Schwonder, attempted to ground his ship, but a rough landing tore off the forward control gondola before she took back to the air. Most of the crew leapt to safety but the wind carried *L.50* away and she was last seen drifting over the Mediterranean with four men still on board. Of the seven airships that did limp back to Germany, one of those, *L.55*, sustained serious damage during a forced landing and had to be dismantled. It had proved a disastrous raid for the Naval Airship Division, with the loss of five Zeppelins. If the gale-force winds had not taken a hand, it probably would have been one of the most successful of the war, for some 78 British aircraft took to the skies in defensive sorties but not one was able to climb high enough to engage the attacking force.

1918: THE END OF THE ZEPPELIN WAR

Even the overtly confident Strasser saw the disastrous outcome of the 19/20 October raid as a major setback. However, the following month new engines became available – designed specifically to combat the strong winds encountered at high altitude – and Strasser's optimism returned. All new airships were to be equipped with the new engine and existing vessels re-fitted. However, before the re-equipped fleet could even contemplate returning to Britain, another disaster struck. On 5 January 1918 a fire broke out at the Ahlhorn airship base – the headquarters of the Naval Airship Division – in one of the massive sheds housing *L.47* and *L.51*. In the great conflagration that followed, the flames engulfed four Zeppelins and one Schütte-Lanz, along with four of the all-important double sheds – effectively putting the base out of service.

Strasser launched only four raids against Britain in 1918, the last year of the war. None of these attempted to target London, choosing instead targets in the Midlands and northern England. The final airship raid took place on

Although *L.45* dropped only a few bombs on the London area, their effect was devastating. The 660 lb bomb that fell in Camberwell demolished 101 and 103 Albany Road and 1 Calmington Road, and severely damaged a great number of others in the area. The bomb killed 10, including Emma, Alice, Stephen and Emily Glass, and injured 23. (Imperial War Museum, HO.113)

5 August 1918. Led by Strasser in person aboard the navy's latest Zeppelin, *L.70*, five airships approached the Norfolk coast. Caught at only 13,000ft, two aircraft of the new amalgamated Royal Air Force pounced on *L.70*. Moments later she 'plunged seaward a blazing mass.' Strasser, the life and soul of the Naval Airship Division, and the driving force behind the raids on Britain, died in action with the rest of the crew.

A SUMMARY OF THE RAIDS

At the start of the war, in both Germany and Britain, belief in the danger of the threat posed to London by the German airships was great. In the early months of the war, London lay exposed, with only a limited defensive capability, but the airship fleet was not in a position to expose this weakness. From May 1915 to the end of the year, the airship raids on London faced little significant opposition, but gradually the defences of the city improved. During 1916, the network of searchlights, anti-aircraft guns and observation posts improved dramatically while the increase in aircraft production further strengthened the defence. Now organized into home defence squadrons with night-flying trained pilots and with the introduction of explosive bullets, from September 1916 the advantage swung dramatically away from the airships. That they kept flying over Britain after this change of circumstances says much for the courage of their officers and crews.

The airship raids on Britain claimed 557 lives and caused injuries to 1,358 men, women and children, with material damage estimated at the time at £1.5 million, with almost £1 million of this inflicted on London. Some 26 raids targeted the capital, but only nine actually reached the central target area. These successful raids killed 181 in the capital and injured 504 people, or 36 per cent of the total casualties.

The aim of the airship raids, to crush the morale of the British population – particularly that of London – and bring about an end to the war, was not achieved. Yet the commitment to home defence tied up vast amounts of weaponry and manpower, preventing their deployment in the front line.

As a weapon of war, the airship was short-lived. But, for all their failure to bring London to its knees, the airships or 'Zepps' as they became known, held a terrible fascination for the civilian population, who viewed them with both awe and horror in equal measure. Despite the passage of time, this haunting fascination still resonates today – long after the greater threat presented by the Gotha and Giant bombers has largely been forgotten.

THE SITES TODAY

The appearance of London has changed much in the 90 years since the end of World War I. The effect of the 1940–41 Blitz and subsequent redevelopment has changed much, but there is still evidence of this first Blitz if you know where to look.

The first bomb dropped on London, by *LZ.38* on 31 May 1915, fell on 16 Alkham Road, Stoke Newington. Despite setting fire to the roof and upstairs rooms, the house still stands. A plaque on the wall of 31 Nevill Road incorrectly identifies it as the first house bombed in the war.

Kapitänleutnant Heinrich Mathy's raid of 8/9 September has also left lasting indicators. A small plaque encircled by paving in one of the central lawns marks the spot where his explosive bomb landed in Queen's Square, Bloomsbury. Moments later another bomb fell outside the Dolphin public house on the corner of Lamb's Conduit Passage and Red Lion Street. The clock in the pub stopped as the bomb exploded and remains in place today, with its hands frozen in time for many years at 22.49. However, in more recent times the hands appear to have slipped to 22.40. Further along the route a plaque on the wall of 61 Farringdon Road commemorates the destruction of that building during the raid.

Another plaque, on the wall of the chapel in Lincoln's Inn, records the explosion of a bomb dropped by Kptlt Breithaupt from *L.15* on 13 October 1915. The bomb shattered the 17th-century stained-glass window while the walls still bear the scars caused by the shrapnel burst.

A number of items relating to the Zeppelin raids are on permanent display at the Imperial War Museum in Lambeth. Perhaps the most interesting is an observation car from Army Zeppelin *LZ.90*, dropped in Essex during the raid of 2/3 September 1916. Another particularly poignant exhibit is Heinrich Mathy's twisted binoculars recovered from the wreck of *L.31*.

Outside London, in Cuffley, Hertfordshire, a monument erected by donations from readers of a national newspaper commemorates William Leefe Robinson's deed in bringing down *SL.11* on the night of 2/3 September 1916, and his subsequent death in 1918. A short distance from Leefe Robinson's grave, in All Saints Church cemetery at Harrow Weald, is the public house called The Leefe Robinson VC, which displays photos and memorabilia connected with the man as well as a few relics recovered from the wreckage of *SL.11*. The crew of *SL.11*, as well as those of three other airship crews brought down over England, now lie in peace in the tranquil setting of the German Military Cemetery at Cannock Chase, Staffordshire.

SELECT BIBLIOGRAPHY

Castle, H.G. *Fire over England* (London, 1982)

Cole, C. and E.F. Cheesman *The Air Defence of Britain, 1914–1918*
(London, 1984)

Fegan, T. *The 'Baby Killers' – German Air Raids on Britain in the First World War*
(Barnsley, 2002)

Griehl, M. and J. Dressel *Zeppelin! – The German Airship Story* (London, 1990)

Jones, H.A. *The War in the Air*, British official history, vol. 3 (London, 1931)

Jones, H.A. *The War In The Air*, British official history, vol. 5 (London, 1935)

Morris, J. *German Air Raids on Britain 1914–1918* (London, 1925 – reprinted
Dallington, 1993)

Poolman, K. *Zeppelins over England* (London,1960)

Rawlinson, A. *The Defence of London, 1915–1918* (London, 1923)

Rimmel, R.L. *Zeppelin! A Battle for Air Supremacy in World War I*
(London, 1984)

Robinson, D.H. *The Zeppelin in Combat* (Atglen, 1994)

Stephenson, C. *Zeppelins: German Airships 1900–40* (Oxford, 2004)

In a separate walled section of the German Military Cemetery at Cannock Chase, the crews of *SL.11*, *L.31*, *L.32* and *L.48* are buried. Their bodies were brought together here in 1966 from Potters Bar, Great Burstead and Theberton.

ORDER OF BATTLE
FOR THE LONDON RAIDS

31 MAY/1 JUNE 1915
GERMAN FORCE
Two German airships

Army Zeppelin LZ.38 (Hptmn Erich Linnarz) – bombed London

Army Zeppelin LZ.37 – returned early

BRITISH DEFENSIVE SORTIES
RNAS – 15 aircraft

Chingford: BE2a, BE2c and Deperdussin

Dover: four aircraft (type unknown)

Eastchurch: Avro 504B, Blériot Parasol, BE2c and Sopwith Tabloid

Hendon: Sopwith Gunbus

Rochford: Blériot Parasol

Westgate: Sopwith Tabloid and Avro 504B

17/18 AUGUST 1915
GERMAN FORCE
Four German airships

Navy Zeppelin L.10 (Oblt-z-S Friedrich Wenke) – bombed London

Navy Zeppelin L.11 – reached England

Navy Zeppelins L.13, L.14 – returned early

BRITISH DEFENSIVE SORTIES
RNAS – 6 aircraft

Chelmsford: Two Caudron G.3

Yarmouth: Sopwith two-seater Scout and two BE2c

Holt: one aircraft (type unknown)

7/8 SEPTEMBER 1915
GERMAN FORCE
Three German airships

Army Schütte-Lanz SL.2 (Hptmn Richard von Wobeser) – bombed London

Army Zeppelin LZ.74 (Hptmn Friedrich George) – bombed London

Army Zeppelin LZ.77 – reached England

BRITISH DEFENSIVE SORTIES
RNAS – 3 aircraft

Felixstowe: BE2c

Yarmouth: BE2c and Sopwith two-seater Scout

8/9 SEPTEMBER 1915
GERMAN FORCE
Three German airships

Navy Zeppelin L.13 (Kptlt Heinrich Mathy) – bombed London

Navy Zeppelins L.9, L.14 – reached England

BRITISH DEFENSIVE SORTIES
RNAS – 7 aircraft

Redcar: Caudron G.3 and two BE2c

Yarmouth: three BE2c

Kingfisher (trawler): Sopwith Schneider (seaplane)

13/14 OCTOBER 1915
GERMAN FORCE
Five German airships

Navy Zeppelin L.13 (Kptlt Heinrich Mathy) – bombed London

Navy Zeppelin L.14 (Kptlt Alois Böcker) – bombed London

Navy Zeppelin L.15 (Kptlt Joachim Breithaupt) – bombed London

Navy Zeppelins L.11, L.16 – reached England

BRITISH DEFENSIVE SORTIES
RFC – 5 aircraft

Joyce Green: two BE2c

Hainault Farm: two BE2c

Suttons Farm: two BE2c

24/25 AUGUST 1916
GERMAN FORCE
Four German airships

Navy Zeppelin L.31 (Kptlt Heinrich Mathy) – bombed London

Navy Zeppelins L.16, L.21, L.32 – reached England

Navy Zeppelins L.14, L.13, L.23 and three others – returned early

Navy Schütte-Lanz SL.8, SL.9 – returned early

BRITISH DEFENSIVE SORTIES
RNAS – 9 aircraft

Eastchurch: two BE2c

Felixstowe: two Short 827

Grain: two BE2c

Manston: BE2c and two Sopwith 1½ Strutter

RFC – 7 aircraft

No. 39 Squadron:

    North Weald: two BE2c

    Suttons Farm: two BE2c

    Hainault Farm: two BE2c

No. 50 Squadron

    Dover: two BE2c

2/3 SEPTEMBER 1916

GERMAN FORCE

16 German airships

Army Schütte-Lanz *SL.11* (Hptmn Wilhelm Schramm) – bombed London

Navy Zeppelins *L.11, L.13, L.14, L.16, L.21, L.22, L.23, L.24, L.30, L.32* – reached England

Navy Schütte Lanz *SL.8* – reached England

Army Zeppelin *LZ.90, LZ.98* – reached England

Army Zeppelin *LZ.97* – returned early

Navy Zeppelin *L.17* – returned early

BRITISH DEFENSIVE SORTIES

RNAS – 4 aircraft

Grain: Farman F.56

Yarmouth: BE2c

Bacton: BE2c

Covehithe: BE2c

RFC – 10 aircraft

No. 33 Squadron:

    Beverley: BE2c

No. 39 Squadron:

    North Weald: BE12 and BE2c

    Suttons Farm: two BE2c

    Hainault Farm: two BE2c

No. 50 Squadron:

    Dover: three BE2c

23/24 SEPTEMBER 1916

GERMAN FORCE

12 German airships

Navy Zeppelin *L.31* (Kptlt Heinrich Mathy) – bombed London

Navy Zeppelin *L.33* (Kptlt Alois Böcker) – bombed London

Navy Zeppelins *L.13, L.14, L.17, L.21, L.22, L.23, L.30, L.32* – reached England

Navy Zeppelins *L.16, L.24* – returned early

BRITISH DEFENSIVE SORTIES

RNAS – 13 aircraft

Cranwell: BE2c

Eastchurch: three BE2c

Manston: two BE2c

Yarmouth: Short 184, two BE2c and two Sopwith Baby

Bacton: BE2c

Covehithe: BE2c

RFC – 12 aircraft

No. 33 Squadron:

    Beverley: BE2c

No. 39 Squadron:

    North Weald: two BE2c

    Suttons Farm: BE2c

    Hainault Farm: two BE2c

No. 50 Squadron:

    Dover: two BE2c

    Bekesbourne: BE2c and one unknown type

No. 51 Squadron:

    Thetford: two aircraft (type unknown)

19/20 OCTOBER 1917

GERMAN FORCE

11 German airships

Navy Zeppelin *L.45* (Kptlt Waldemar Kölle) – bombed London

Navy Zeppelins *L.41, L.44, L.46, L.47, L.49, L.50, L.52, L.53, L.54, L.55* – reached England

BRITISH DEFENSIVE SORTIES

RNAS –11 aircraft

Cranwell: BE2e

Frieston: BE2c

Manston: three BE2c

Yarmouth: BE2c

Bacton: BE2c

Burgh Castle: three BE2c

Covehithe: BE2c

RFC – 66 aircraft

No. 33 Squadron:

    Scampton: two FE2b and three FE2d

    Kirton-Lindsey: three FE2b and three FE2d

    Elsham: two FE2d

    Gainsborough: FE2d and FE2b

No. 37 Squadron:

    Goldhanger: BE2d, two BE2e and BE12

    Stow Maries: four BE2e

No. 38 Squadron:

    Leadenham: two FE2b

    Buckminster: two FE2b

    Stamford: four FE2b

No. 39 Squadron:

    North Weald: seven BE2e and Martinsyde G.102 (attached)

    Biggin Hill: BE2c, BE12 and BE12a

No. 50 Squadron:

    Bekesbourne: BE2e and three BE12

No. 51 Squadron:

    Mattishall: two FE2b

    Tydd St Mary: two FE2b

    Marham: two FE2b

No. 75 Squadron:

    Hadleigh: three BE2e and BE12

    Harling Road: two BE2e and BE12

    Elmswell: BE2e

No. 76 Squadron:

    Copmanthorpe: three BE2e and BE12

    Helperby: BE2e and BE12

INDEX

Figures in **bold** refer to illustrations.